WHAT YOU SHOULD KNOW ABOUT THE

GOLDEN DAWN

Other Controversial Titles From New Falcon

Undoing Yourself With Energized Meditation
Secrets of Western Tantra
The Tree of Lies
  All By Christopher S. Hyatt, Ph.D.
The Enochian World of Aleister Crowley
  By Aleister Crowley, L. M. DuQuette, and C. S. Hyatt
The Way of The Secret Lover
  By Christopher S. Hyatt , Ph.D. and Lon M. DuQuette
Aleister Crowley's Illustrated Goetia: Sexual Evocation
  By C. S. Hyatt, L. M. DuQuette and D. Wilson
Pacts With The Devil
  By S. J. Black and Christopher. S. Hyatt, Ph.D.
Urban Voodoo
  By Christopher. S. Hyatt, Ph.D. and S. J. Black
Equinox of the Gods
Eight Lectures on Yoga
Gems From the Equinox
Little Essays Toward Truth
Heart of the Master
Magick Without Tears
Temple of Solomon The King
  All By Aleister Crowley
Neuropolitique
Info-Psychology
Game of Life
  All By Timothy Leary, Ph.D.
Zen Without Zen Masters
  By Camden Benares
Cosmic Trigger: The Final Secret Of The Illuminati
Cosmic Trigger II: Down To Earth
Prometheus Rising
  All By Robert Anton Wilson, Ph.D.
The Complete Golden Dawn System of Magic
What You Should Know About The Golden Dawn
The Eye In The Triangle
Healing Energy, Prayer and Relaxation
Golden Dawn Tapes—Series I, II and III
  All By Israel Regardie

And to get a free catalog of *all* of our titles, write to:

NEW FALCON PUBLICATIONS (Catalog Dept.)
655 East Thunderbird
Phoenix, AZ 85022 U.S.A.

WHAT YOU SHOULD KNOW
ABOUT THE
GOLDEN
DAWN

BY
ISRAEL REGARDIE

FOREWORD BY
Christopher S. Hyatt, Ph.D.

1993
NEW FALCON PUBLICATIONS
PHOENIX, ARIZONA, USA

International Standard Book Number: 0-56184-064-5
Library of Congress Catalog Card Number: 83-81663

First Edition 1936
Second Printing 1971

Third Edition (revised) 1983 Falcon Press
Fourth Printing 1985

Fifth Edition (enlarged) 1988
Sixth Printing 1993

New Falcon Publications
655 East Thunderbird
Phoenix, Arizona 85022 U.S.A.

CONTENTS

LIST OF ERRATA

Page 15. 4th line from the bottom, last word "with" should be "within"
39. 3rd. Delete "s" from "Obligations."
28th. First word should be plural "poseurs."
31st. "dubious" not "budious."
56. 28th. Substitute comma for period. Delete "And" after origin and insert "then."
58. 4th line from bottom. Delete last "e" in employes.
68. 17th. Delete "one of."
72. 3rd. "Portal" not "portal."
32nd. "Commit" not comit."
82. 25th. "animo" should be "anima."
83. 14th. "Tipharath" should be "Tiphareth."
87. 11th. "Offiice" should be "office."
88. 10th. "are" should be "were."
99. 15th. "about" should be "above."
102. 24th. "indentical;; should be "identical."
107. 17th. "was" should be "is."
109. 9th. "incrustions" should be "instructions."
126. 5th. "Adeptum" should be "Adeptus."
134. 11th. "srongly" should be "strongly."
135. 1st. Insert after "casts" the following. "of the Kerubim, the holy animals of Ezekiel's Vision the head of a lion, an eagle, a"
139. 5th. "then" should be "the."
140. 6th. Before "perfect" insert "the."

FOREWORD

O Agni, Holy Fire! Purifying Fire! You who sleep in the wood, and ascend in Shining flames on the altar, you are the heart of sacrifice, the fearless wings of prayer, the divine Spark hidden in everything, and the glorious soul of the sun!

Vedic Hymn

THE RITE OF SPRING

At times I have summed up the Golden Dawn in one sentence, it is -- The Rite of Spring -- the period of the sacramental transmutation of the person who has dwelt in darkness into one who now lives in light. Like Buddhism and Gnostic Christianity, the Golden Dawn has no doctrine of substitutional enlightenment, atonement or redemption. Attainment (Enlightenment) rests upon one's own work and effort.

THE PURPOSE OF THE GOLDEN DAWN

The purpose of the Golden Dawn is to raise the aspirant to a level of "More than Human," so as to enable him to have the conversation with his "Higher Self." This is accomplished through a series of "learning experiences," the acquisition of states of higher consciousness and initiation. The initiation experience can be likened to the birth process, to quote Israel Regardie, "Initiation means to begin, to start something new. It represents the beginning of a new life dedicated to an entirely different set of principles than those. . .held by 'homo normalis.' Initiation is the preparation for immortality. Man is only *potentially* immortal. Immortality is acquired when the purely human part of him

VII

becomes allied to that spiritual essence which was never created, was never born, and shall never die. It is to effect this spiritual bond with the highest, that the Golden Dawn owes its ritual and practical magical work." (*The Complete Golden Dawn System of Magic, 1984, Falcon Press.*) To sum this up, initiation is not a fantasy or delusion as some wish to think; but the fashioning, the forming of the soul through itself.

What is it that keeps normal man away from the true knowledge of his Higher Self? To put it another way, what stands between man and his God? There are no simple answers. Those of us on the path know that we "live in" the Divine Self, and it "lives in" us. In truth there is really no separation. If this is the case, why then do so few "attain?" Again there is no simple answer. There appears to be *a veil, a sheath, a film*, which separates us from **the knowledge** and **conversation** of the Divine Self. This *film* or covering is very thin, yet very tenacious. It has been said that if we could just remember "who and what we are" between each breath the *film* would dissolve. I think the poet here was not simply using metaphor but describing a process. The unredeemed man is asleep "forever fixed in his preoccupations." He flounders in his unconsciousness believing all the time that he is awake.

The process of transformation first requires that the sleeping self must be awakened. We might describe this as a "calling." Who is doing the "calling?" The force which "calls" is the Higher Self. The methods of "calling" are numerous, however, the most common is pain. It is paradoxical, but, that which man dislikes most (pain) is frequently the experience which gives him the first glimpse of the Higher Self. It is said that "many are called but few are chosen." Why is this? First, I believe the rigours of preparation finally separates the gold from the dross. If one knew at the beginning what was involved in "attaining," few would proceed further. Luckily most of us do not know in the beginning what is required of us. As we proceed and begin to find out, we reach a point of no-return. At this point there is no-going back. Instead of the Great Work being a part of our life -- it becomes the center of our life. Instead of remaining ego-centric we become Self-centric. Once this happens we are transformed. The setting Sun is devoured by the Sea, fertilized and pregnant, bringing forth the New Sun -- The Golden Dawn.

Second, many initiating organizations in their outcry for number not require much from their aspirants. In the worlds preoccupation with materialism it is accepted proverbially that few have the time, money or the inclination to do "what is necessary" to "achieve." Compare many of our modern initiatory organizations with that of the Eygptians at the time of Rameses. The ancient initiation based itself on the wholism of mind (soul), body, and spirit. The priests of Rameses time demanded a "re-working" of the entire human being. This was a slow and painstaking process. However, when mastery was achieved it was not in name alone. Are we again about to see a re-birth of this wholistic spirit?

THE REBIRTH OF MAGIC

According to Francis King in his most illuminating book *The Rebirth of Magic,* "It is only since the 1950's that the Western Magical revival, that long drawn out process of occult evolution begun by Eliphas Levi over a century and a quarter ago, has come to the attention of the general public. Over the last 25 or so years there has been an occult boom, a magical explosion,' of a sort not experienced since the later years of the Roman Empire. To give a detailed account of this cultural revolution would require many thousands -- perhaps many tens of thousands -- of words. All that we can even begin to do in one short chapter is to outline the achievements of some of those contemporary occultists who have either played a major part in the occult revival, or in one way or another, typify certain aspects of it.

That the rebirth of occult magic has taken place in the way it has can be very largely attributed to the writings of one man, Dr. Francis Israel Regardie. It is not, of course, that all magicians approve of Dr. Regardie and his opinions - indeed some of them have an antipathetic attitude towards him and them. Nevertheless, there would be far, far fewer practising Western occultists working in either the Golden Dawn or Crowleyan' traditions if Dr. Regardie had never written any books."

I believe that Mr. King's view of the rebirth of magic is no understatement. Furthermore I hold with his opinion that without Israel Regardie or someone like him "there would be far, far fewer practising Western occultists. . ." When Falcon Press first published *What You Should Know About The Golden Dawn* in 1983, *The Complete Golden Dawn System Of Magic* was not yet released. Although Falcon Press had been promising Regardie's Magnum Opus since 1982 it did not appear until the summer of 1984. The work was beset with one delay or difficulty after another. Besides the immense effort involved, the costs to produce such a work for such a "young press" were enormous. Rumors of Regardie's death and Falcon Press' "death" were rampant. Finally, the "call" from the bindery came and the book was released. The point of this discussion is that not only has there been a re-birth of magic per se, but there has been a re-birth of the Golden Dawn. This is evident by a number of factors. First was the praiseful response which Regardie and Falcon Press received from the occult community at large. Second, was the number of letters which we received asking us for information regarding joining the Golden Dawn. Thirdly, the knowledge that the number of working Temples in the United States is increasing.

THE REBIRTH OF THE GOLDEN DAWN

In order to aid in the dissemination of the knowledge that *The Complete Golden Dawn System of Magic* offers, the USESS has established a *Golden Dawn Temple and Society*. We are pleased to say that membership is now open. We are in no way affiliated with any Temple now operating in the World, nor do we have any control over these Temples. Our major purpose is to offer opportunities for Initiation and Certification to those students who are willing to demonstrate their dedication and committment to the Great Work. Those individuals who show a sincere aptitude for self-actualization will have their work examined and duly certified. We believe that much of the preparatory work can be done by the student without the need for a local temple (See Volume I pages 8-12 in *The Complete Golden Dawn System of Magic*). The Golden Dawn Temple and Society will provide guidance through consultation, examination and net-working. In the near future we plan to have an operating Temple and Sanctuary, where aspirants can come to study and receive Initiation. Opportunities to participate in upcoming workshops will be made available to those who wish to study and prepare themself in all aspects of "esoteric religion." Finally the Golden Dawn Temple and Society in affiliation with Falcon Press will be offering book club for members in good standing. For further information write to me personally, or to the Golden Dawn Temple and Society C/ Falcon Press 3660 N. 3rd. St. Phoenix Az. 85012.

A NOTE ON THE COMPLETE GOLDEN DAWN SYSTEM

The Complete Golden Dawn System of Magic is the major source of western magical knowledge. In my view it is the only magical gnosis of any real worth that the West has known. This enlarged edition can do nothing but encourage the student on his path to Enlightenment. However as Regardie has warned and has emphasized to me over and

X

over again, "the emotional makeup of the student must be purified before the real and true benefits of the Golden Dawn can find a true and lasting home." For several decades he has asserted that the best preparation for the pursuit of magic is a course of therapy. I fully concur with Regardie, particularly when I have had first hand opportunity to view the results obtained by those who didn't heed his warning. I would like to share an observation which I have seen over and over again. Perhaps the most obvious and the most dangerous problem is an overwhelming increase in ego-centricity. Instead of the Magical work producing the desired effect of shifting the focus of energy from ego-centeredness to Self-centeredness, the God-like universal and impersonal power of the Self is claimed by the ego as its own creation. When this happens all true progress ceases. It is as if a substitution takes place; the student appears as if "he personally" "him alone" (IS) the Divine force. His desires and whims are paramount, any threat to his personal authority are met with venomous attacks. I have found that this *can be* avoided by a course in therapy as well as keeping in mind the following "be prompt and active as the Sylphs, but avoid frivolity and caprice. Be energetic and strong as the Salamanders, but avoid irritability and ferocity. Be flexible and attentive to images, like the Undines, but avoid idleness and changeability. Be laborious and patient like the Gnomes, but avoid grossness and avarice. So shalt thou gradually develop the powers of thy soul and fit thyself to command the spirits of the elements."

With this aside -- let us all strive to quit the darkness that has blinded us from our true and ineffable Self and Seek the White Light which stands before us -- now.

C.S. Hyatt
Los Angeles
Revised March 1985

XI

INTRODUCTION TO THE THIRD EDITION

Sometime after the writing of the Introduction to the Second Edition to this book, there appeared on the scene *The Magicians of the Golden Dawn* by Ellic Howe. Its intent was to investigate the background data relating to the founders of the Golden Dawn and the Order itself. It was supposed to be an entirely objective history.

I received my first letter from Mr. Howe in December 1969. Others were written before the publication of his book. In these letters, he stated what he repeated in the book itself -- that he is not an occultist nor a magician, but primarily an objective historian probing into various underground movements. At first, I accepted that information on its face value; I had no reason then to question that statement. At his suggestion, I obtained a copy of an earlier book of his dealing with the historical usage of astrology in England and then abroad in Europe. In that book first published in England as *Urania's Children* and then in the United States as *Astrology: a Recent History including the untold story of its Role in World War II,* he varies the above quoted definition of his role by remarking that he is not an astrologer but simply an investigator, though in that book he speaks of "the incomprehensible technical jargon" in some of the books and magazines he had read. I invite Mr. Howe to read a couple of books on chemistry I have, one on Biochemistry and another on Laboratory Diagnosis. If they are not at first reading as mysterious and as incomprehensible as the astrological material he derides, I am willing to eat my hat. His prejudice is palpable.

However, one of the *pieces de resistance* in this writer's so-called objectivity is to be found on page 73, especially in a footnote which states that "Modern Cabalistic works by such occultists as Dion Fortune *The Mystical Qabalah* (1935) and Israel Regardie, *The Tree of Life,* (1932), can be safely ignored." Most modern authorities on his subject would laugh him to scorn -- and so do I.

There is a rather amusing aside to this matter. Shortly after Riders publication of *The Tree of Life* in 1932, the *London Saturday Review* reviewed it under the heading of "The Way of Madness" by a Student of Life. Its author was really the editor, H. Warner Allen.

In the 10 Dec. 1932 issue of that same journal, the editor did have the decency and courage to publish a letter from a medical psychologist condemning the review and offering his own comments, as follows:

"Having read with the greatest possible interest and approval *The Tree of Life* by Israel Regardie, I was surprised by the lack of insight shown in his criticism by 'A Student of Life.' Largely by the experience of patients and of my own, and a little by the study of the written works of others, I have gradually discovered a little about life. It was with amazement and the joy of meeting a friend in a strange land that I read Mr. Regardie's book and found that the little I had discovered was a very small part of that very elaborate system which he has enunciated in his book with so much simplicity. My own method has always been the scientific one, and I was deeply impressed that his was the same, but where I was only a beginner he has shown me the way to further progress in my search for understanding.

Your reviewer is confused and unfair, but Mr. Regardie is neither. I write hoping that the intelligent reader may not be put off by an unintelligent review from reading a work of great significance and value. It is not one which can be readily appreciated by all because of the inherent difficulty of its subject, but there are many to whom it would come as a ray of light on a dark road."

The psychiatrist was E. Graham Howe, M.D., and as it turned out Mr. Ellic Howe told me when corresponding that the former was his uncle. It is too bad the good "hokum-buster" did not take counsel of his uncle before, during or after he wrote his book *The Magicians of the Golden Dawn*, or the stupid footnotes in his astrology critique. Dr. Graham Howe might have been able to teach his blind prejudiced nephew a thing or two.

I reviewed his book *The Magicians of the Golden Dawn* sometime after publication in as derogatory way as I possibly could, since I smelled prejudice and ridicule on every page. This review apparently was read as far afield as Japan for in April 1973, I received a letter from a European living in Kamakura, Japan, in which he stated:

XIV

"Mr. Ellic Howe disclaims any personal involvement with occultism and says that he is only a 'historian of ideas'." I got to wonder again. I have here a copy of his lecture delivered on September 14, 1972 about *Fringe Masonry in England 1870-1885* as reprinted in the Transactions of the A.Q.C. Vol. 85 (1972). The date indicates that he was well toward finishing his book on the Golden Dawn. For good measure, let me quote the very beginning of that lecture:

"My first encounter with the concept of 'fringe' Masonry and the names of Kenneth MacKenzie and Francis George Irwin was in 1961 when I was baffled by almost everything relating to the origins and early history of Dr. W. Wynn Westcott's extraordinary androgynous magical society, the Hermetic Order of the Golden Dawn. A.E. Waite suggested in his autobiographical *Shadows of Life and Thought* 1938) that Mackenzie might once have owned the Golden Dawn's legendary Cypher Manuscripts, although this seems unlikely. The provenance of this document is unknown and likely to remain so. It was in the possession of the Rev. A.F.A. Woodford, a founder member of the Q.C. Lodge, in 1886, and he gave it to Westcott in August 1887. Thereafter we are confronted with a lunatic story of fabricated letters, Invisible Chiefs and, for good measure, the introduction of a mythical German lady called Fraulein Sprengel, otherwise the Greatly Honoured Soror Sapiens Dominabitur Astris, allegedly an eminent "Rosicrucian" adept. It was she according to Westcott, who gave him permission to operate the Golden Dawn in this country. While all this is great fun for amateurs of the absurd, it is outside the scope of this paper."

My correspondent in Japan added, "He does, however, come back to the G.D. several times during this lecture. This statement of Mr. Ellic Howe makes it rather clear how 'unbiased' he is regarding the G.D."

My review was published in *Gnostica News* (Llewellyns, St. Paul) on January 21, 1974, and for the sake of relative completeness I suggest to those interested to find a copy of the review and read it in this light.

In this connection, the interested reader should also consult a couple of other books which have as their primary object the debunking of occultism, making them companions of that written by Ellic Howe. While it is true that some phases of the subject do need debunking to get rid of the wholly irrational and sensational elements, a great deal of care and first hand knowledge is evidently required to handle the subject fairly and honestly. The books referred to are *The Occult Underground* and *The Occult Establishment* by James Webb (Open Court Publishing Co., La Salle, Ill., 1976 and 1974). I found both of these books fascinating and intriguing, with much that I concurred with. Yet there was the same kind of apparent objectivity covering up a mass of errors and prejudice that were quite palpable.

I would like to see one of the younger brethren, as it were, with more time than I and more of a penchant for research and polemics, to take both these books apart and destroy their appeal to those who feel they must thoroughly wipe out all traces of legitimate occultism and mysticism.

Israel Regardie
Phoenix, Arizona
May 1982

CHAPTER ONE

THE GOLDEN DAWN

"The Order of the Golden Dawn," narrates the history lecture of that Order, "is an Hermetic Society whose members are taught the principles of Occult Science and the Magic of Hermes. During the early part of the second half of last century, several eminent Adepti and Chiefs of the Order in France and England died, and their death caused a temporary dormant condition of Temple work.

"Prominent among the Adepti of our Order and of public renown, were Eliphas Levi the greatest of modern French magi; Ragon, the author of several books of occult lore; Kenneth M. Mackenzie, author of the famous and learned Masonic Encyclopaedia; and F r e d e r i c k Hockley possessed of the power of vision in the crystal, and whose manuscripts are highly esteemed. These and other contemporary Adepti of this Order received their knowledge and power from predecessors of equal and even of greater eminence. They received indeed and have handed down to us their doctrine and system of Theosophy and Hermetic Science and the higher Alchemy from a long series of practised investigators whose origin is traced to the Fratres Roseae Crucis of Germany, which association was founded by one Christian Rosenkreutz about the year 1398 A. D. . . .

"The Rosicrucian revival of Mysticism was but a new development of the vastly older wisdom of the Qabalistic Rabbis and of that very ancient secret knowledge, the Magic of the Egyptians, in which the Hebrew Pentateuch tells you that Moses the founder of the Jewish system was 'learned', that is, in which he had been initiated."

7

In a slender but highly informative booklet entitled *Data of the History of the Rosicrucians* published in 1916 by the late Dr. William Wynn Westcott, we find the following brief statement: "In 1887 by permission of S.D.A. a continental Rosicrucian Adept, the Isis-Urania Temple of Hermetic Students of the G. D. was formed to give instruction in the mediaeval Occult sciences. Fratres M.E.V. with S.A. and S.R.M.D. became the chiefs, and the latter wrote the rituals in modern English from old Rosicrucian mss. (the property of S.A.) supplemented by his own literary researches."

In these two statements is narrated the beginning of the Hermetic Order of the Golden Dawn—an organisation which has exerted a greater influence on the development of Occultism since its revival in the last quarter of the 19th century than most people can realise. There can be little or no doubt that the Golden Dawn is, or rather was until very recently, the sole depository of magical knowledge, the only Occult Order of any real worth that the West in our time has known, and a great many other occult organisations owe what little magical knowledge is theirs to leakages issuing from that Order and from its renegade members.

The membership of the Golden Dawn was recruited from every circle, and it was represented by dignified professions as well as by all the arts and sciences, to make but little mention of the trades and business occupations. It included physicians, psychologists, clergymen, artists and philosophers; and normal men and women, humble and unknown, from every walk of life have drawn inspiration from its font of wisdom, and undoubtedly many would be happy to recognise and admit the enormous debt they owe to it.

As an organisation, it preferred always to shroud itself in an impenetrable cloak of mystery. Its teaching and methods of instruction were stringently guarded by various penalties attached to the most awe-inspiring obligations in order to ensure that secrecy. So well have these obligations with but one or two exceptions been kept that the general public knows next to nothing about the Order, its teaching, or the extent and nature of its membership. Though this book will touch upon the teaching of the Golden Dawn, concerning its membership as a whole the writer will have nothing to say, except perhaps to repeat what may already be more or less well-known. For instance, it is common knowledge that W. B. Yeats, Arthur Machen and, if rumour may be trusted, the late Arnold Bennett were at one time among its members, together with a good many other writers and artists.

With regard to the names given in Dr. Westcott's statement it is necessary that we bestow to them some little attention in order to unravel, so far as may be possible, the almost inextricable confusion which has characterised every previous effort to detail the history of the Order. M.E.V. was the motto chosen by Dr. William Robert Woodman, an eminent Freemason of the last century. Sapere Aude and Non Omnis Moriar were the two mottos used by Dr. Westcott, an antiquarian, scholar, and coroner by profession. S.R.M.D. or S. Rhiogail Ma Dhream was the motto of S.L. MacGregor Mathers, the translator of *The Greater Key of King Solomon*, the *Book of the Sacred Magic of Abramelin the Mage*, and *The Qabalah Unveiled*, which latter consisted of certain portions of the Zohar prefixed by an introduction of high erudition. He also employed the Latin motto Deo Duce Comite Ferro. S. D. A. was the abbreviation of the motto Sapiens Dominabitur Astris chosen by a Fräulein Anna Sprengel of Nüremberg, Germany. Such were the actors on this occult stage, this the *dramatis personae* in the background of the commencement of the Order. More than any other figures who may later have prominently figured in its government and work, these are the four

9

outstanding figures publicly involved in the English foundation of what came to be known as The Hermetic Order of the Golden Dawn.

How the actual beginning came to pass is not really known. Or rather, because of so many conflicting stories and legends the truth is impossible to discover. At any rate, so far as England is concerned, without a doubt we must seek for its origins in the Societas Rosicruciana in Anglia. This was an organisation formulated in 1865 by eminent Freemasons, some of them claiming Rosicrucian initiation from continental authorities. Amongst those who claimed such initiation was one Kenneth Mackenzie, a Masonic scholar and encyclopaedist, who had received his at the hands of a Count Apponyi in Austria. The objects of this Society which confined its membership to Freemasons in good standing, was "to afford mutual aid and encouragement in working out the great problems of Life, and in discovering the secrets of nature; to facilitate the study of the systems of philosophy founded upon the Kaballah and the doctrines of Hermes Trismegistus." Dr. Westcott also remarks that to-day its Fratres "are concerned in the study and administration of medicines, and in their manufacture upon old lines; they also teach and practise the curative effects of coloured light, and cultivate mental processes which are believed to induce spiritual enlightenment and extended powers of the human senses, especially in the directions of clairvoyance and clairaudience."

The first Chief of this Society, its Supreme Magus so-called, was one Robert Wentworth Little, who is said to have rescued some old rituals from a certain Masonic storeroom, and it was from certain of those papers that the Society's rituals were elaborated. He died in 1878, and in his stead was appointed Dr. William R. Woodman. Both Dr. Westcott and MacGregor Mathers were prominent and active members of this body. In fact, the

10

former became Supreme Magus upon Woodman's death, the office of Junior Magus being conferred upon Mathers. One legend has it that one day Westcott discovered in his library a series of cipher manuscripts, and in order to decipher them he enlisted the aid of MacGregor Mathers. It is said that this library was that of the Societas Rosicruciana in Anglia, and it is likewise asserted that those cipher manuscripts were among the rituals and documents originally rescued by Robert Little from Freemason's Hall. Yet other accounts have it that Westcott found the manuscripts on a bookstall in Farringdon Street. Further apocryphal legends claim that they were found in the library of books and manuscripts inherited from the mystic and clairvoyant, Frederick Hockley who died in 1885. Whatever the real origin of these mysterious cipher manuscripts, when eventually deciphered with the aid of MacGregor Mathers, they were alleged to have contained the address of Fräulein Anna Sprengel who purported to be a Rosicrucian Adept, in Nüremburg. Here was a discovery which, naturally, not for one moment was neglected. Its direct result was a lengthy correspondence with Fräulein Sprengel, culminating in the transmission of authority to Woodman, Westcott and Mathers, to formulate in England a semi-public occult organisation which was to employ an elaborate magical ceremonial, Qabalistic teaching, and a comprehensive scheme of spiritual training. Its foundation was designed to include both men and women on a basis of perfect equality in contradistinction to the policy of the Societas Rosicruciana in Anglia which was comprised wholly of Freemasons. Thus, in 1887, the Hermetic Order of the Golden Dawn was established. Its first English Temple, Isis-Urania, was opened in the following year.

There is a somewhat different version as to its origin, having behind it the authority of Frater F. R. the late Dr. Felkin, who was the Chief of the Stella Matutina as well as a member of the Societas Rosicruciana. According to his account, and the following words are substantially his own, prior to 1880 members of the Rosicrucian Order on the Continent selected with great care their own candidates whom they thought suitable for personal instruction. For these pupils they were each individually responsible, the pupils thus selected being trained by them in the theoretical traditional knowledge now used in the Outer Order. After some three or more years of intensive private study they were presented to the Chiefs of the Order, and if approved and passed by examination, they then received their initiation into the Order of the Roseae Rubeae et Aureae Crucis.

The political state of Europe in those days was such that the strictest secrecy as to the activities of these people was very necessary. England, however, where many Masonic bodies and semi-private organisations were flourishing without interference, was recognised as having far greater freedom and liberty than the countries in which the continental Adepts were domiciled. Some, but by no means all, suggested therefore that in England open Temple work might be inaugurated. And Dr. Felkin here adds, though without the least word of explanation as to what machinery was set in motion towards the attainment of that end, "and so it was . . . . It came about then that Temples arose in London, Bradford, Weston-super-Mare, and Edinburgh. The ceremonies we have were elaborated from cipher manuscripts, and all went well for a time."

As to what ensued after that inauguration of Temple work here we have little record, though an unorthodox account written by Aleister Crowley continues this historical theme in substantially the same words as were orally communicated to me by the late Imperator of one of the now-existent Temples. "After some time S.D.A. died; further requests for help were met with a prompt

12

refusal from the colleagues of S.D.A. It was written by one of them that S.D.A.'s schemes had always been regarded with disapproval but since the absolute rule of the Adepts is never to interfere with the judgment of any other person whomsoever—how much more, then, one of themselves, and that one most highly revered!—they had refrained from active opposition. The Adept who wrote this added that the Order had already quite enough knowledge to enable it or its members to formulate a magical link with the adepts. Shortly after this, one called S.R.M.D. announced that he had formulated such a link, and that himself with two others was to govern the Order . . . . We content ourselves, then, with observing that the death of one of his two colleagues, and the weakness of the other, secured to S.R.M.D., the sole authority . . . . "

In elaboration of this statement, it may be said that in 1891 Dr. Woodman died after but a few days illness, leaving the management of the Order to Westcott and Mathers. Evidently these two scholars carried on quite well together for about six years, for the indications are that the Order flourished and grew expansive. Exactly why Westcott withdrew from the Order—for this is the next major occurrence—appears difficult to discover. Concerning this also several versions are extant. One account has it that accidentally he left some of the Order manuscripts in a portfolio bearing his signature in a cab, and the driver upon finding them turned them over to the authorities. Since Westcott was by profession an East London coroner, the medical authorities strongly objected that one in an official capacity should, no matter how remotely, be connected with anything that savoured occult. It was suggested to him therefore that he must withdraw from the Order or else resign his post as coroner, since the two were considered in those days incompatibles. He chose to resign from the Order. Yet again it is suggested

13

that it was simply a personal quarrel that led to the parting of the ways with Mathers, which does seem the more probable explanation. Whatever the cause, some six years after the death of Dr. Woodman, Westcott withdrew from the Order, which was thus left to the sole authority of Mathers.

The pamphlet on Rosicrucian history then proceeds in narrative that following Westcott's resignation from "this association in 1897, the English Temples soon after fell into abeyance." This reads like an instance of wish-fulfilment. Though fairly near the essential truth of the matter, it is not quite in accordance with fact. Following the resignation of Westcott, Mathers reigned within his Order as supreme autocrat. Judging from the evidence at our disposal he was not a particularly benevolent one, for many were the misunderstandings that ruffled the mystic placidity of his Temples, and several of the individuals who dared so much as to differ or argue with him were promptly expelled, and flung into the outer darkness. Presumably spiritual pride was the flaw in his armour, and he seemed to harbour quite a few delusions. One of the latter was his conveyance to the body of Adepti as a piece of objective everyday experience, that whilst in the Bois de Boulogne one day he was approached by three Adepts who confirmed him in the sole rulership of the Order. On the strength of this supposed occurrence, he issued to the Theorici of the grade of Adeptus Minor a powerfully worded manifesto, naming himself in no uncertain terms as a chosen vessel and demanding from all those who received the manifesto a signed oath of personal loyalty and allegiance. Those who refused to send a written statement of voluntary submission to him were either expelled from the Order or degraded to a lower rank.

Meanwhile, a considerable amount of discontent had been slowly brewing amongst the Order members. Dis-

14

satisfaction with the autocratic leadership of S.R.M.D. was growing very steadily and persistently. No definite or clear-cut reasons appear to be given for this, for evidently this restlessness had been gradually fructifying whilst the hypertrophy of Mathers' ego was becoming more and more pronounced. Some say that S.R.M.D. was guilty of innumerable magical tricks of a particularly irresponsible nature which eventually brought disrepute both upon himself and the Order of which he was head. Others, more romantically minded, claimed that his English translation of *The Sacred Magic of Abramelin the Mage* was a powerful magical act which attracted to his sphere forces of evil so terrible in nature that he was wholly unable to withstand them. Frater F.R. propounds the more rational view that it was simply spiritual pride and love of power which so gained the ascendancy that he demanded of the members of his organisation a personal fealty and obedience to his own personality instead of to the work itself. How very familiar all this sounds? In one form or another, it is the story of the same unhappy fate which dogs and finally ruins every religious and spiritual community. By changing these names, Theosophists may recognise a very homely story.

In claiming his right to unquestioned leadership, and when refusing to appoint two others of the body of Adepti to fill the vacant posts of co-Chiefs, Mathers also promised some of the more advanced members of the Second Order additional grades in the path of Adeptship and even more esoteric teaching. These, apparently, were not forthcoming—though it must be confessed that regardless of the personal shortcomings of Mathers as a leader or as a writer, it is patent that there was a vast knowledge and a deep and wide erudition concealed with him. Naturally the Adepti gave utterance to their complete disapproval of this delay in the fulfilment of their Chief's promises, gradually coming to insist that he had neither the knowledge nor the grades to impart. Further unpleasant bickering drew forth from Mathers the retort that he was certainly not going to waste either his grades or knowledge on such hopeless duffers as they were. And in any event, he was Chief and leader; their further progress, if there was to be any, must be left entirely in his hands. In short, a virulent quarrel was in process of development, and though for quite a long time it fermented beneath the surface, it finally culminated in a group of the Adepti forming a strong combination to expel their chief S.R.M.D. Just prior to the actual appearance of the schism, and whilst yet the rebellion was gaining impetus, certain events happened which call here not for elucidation, since that is impossible, but simply for registration.

About this time, a certain Mrs. Rose Horos approached Mathers who came to acknowledge her as an initiate of a high grade. Exactly why, it is again impossible to say definitely. It was stated in defence of Mathers that Mrs. Horos was able to repeat to him a certain conversation he had had years previously when he visited Madame Blavatsky at Denmark Hill, and the repetition of this scrap of conversation convinced him of her status. Anyway, it was a sad piece of deception, and an unhappy acknowledgment on the part of Mathers indicating his complete lack of judgment and insight into character. Mrs. Horos and her husband were very soon discovered to be sexperverts of the worst description. Nor was this all, for it is alleged that they were also responsible for the theft from Mathers of a complete set of Order documents. It seems incredible that Mathers could have been so gullible, for that is the only word which adequately describes his stupidity, as to accept without further verification the occult claims of this woman, giving her access to the rituals and teaching of the Golden Dawn. Subsequently the immoral activities of these two people having attracted the attention of the police, they were arrested. In Decem-

16

ber 1901 at their trial, the Order of the Golden Dawn was given unpleasant and unjustified publicity by being associated with the chequered careers of these two persons. In the witness box the male prisoner made the remark concerning the Golden Dawn Neophyte obligation that it "was prepared by the Chiefs of the Order who are in India"—which of course was a farrago of nonsense, but unfortunately just the type of nonsense which survives for many years. He was sentenced to fifteen years penal servitude, and his wife to seven.

Around this period also, one Florence Farr, whose esoteric motto was Soror S.S.D.D., having for some years been left in charge of Isis-Urania Temple while Mathers continued his research work in Paris, decided for various personal reasons to enter her resignation from that important post. Under date of February 16th 1900, Mathers, writing from Paris, refused to accept her resignation, believing that she intended to "form a combination to make a schism therein with the idea of working secretly or avowedly under Sapere Aude." In this same letter, he was responsible for the astonishing statement that S.A. had never been at any time in touch with Fräulein Sprengel of Nüremburg but had "either himself forged or procured to be forged the professed correspondence between him and her." As was only to be expected this letter came as a overwhelming surprise to S.S.D.D., who was thoroughly stunned by this accusation of dishonesty and forgery levelled against S.A. After contemplating the whole situation in an almost frantic state of mind for several days in the country, she finally communicated with S.A. asking him to corroborate or deny the accusations. Her next act was to form a Committee of Seven within the Second Order to investigate the allegations made. This Committee asked S.R.M.D. to produce for his own sake and for the sake of the Order proof of the accuracy of his statements. Because, they argued, since it was upon the authority of this alleged correspondence that the Order was founded, the historical position of the Order as descended from mediaeval Rosicrucian sources collapsed should it be proven that the correspondence had been forged. This viewpoint was not altogether accurate, for while S.R.M.D. had stated that S.A. had never been in touch with S.D.A., he never denied that he himself had not been in constant communication with her. Then followed a lengthy correspondence which afterwards was collected and printed in the form of a long dossier. In fine, Mathers refused unconditionally to acknowledge the authority or even the existence of the Committee nor would he produce proof of any kind to substantiate his claim that S.A., had forged Second Order communications. It goes without saying of course that S.A. fervently denied the truth of these allegation of forgery, but all the same he refused to do anything about it.

No good purpose could possibly be served by enlarging upon the unhappy events which immediately followed. To a large extent the history of the Order is so confused and muddled at this juncture, and the rumours which have come down to us so chaotic and contradictory, that it has proved wholly impossible to extricate the truth from the foul débris of slander, abuse and recrimination. A clear picture of what occurred seems impossible to recover. It would appear, to state the matter simply, that Mathers expelled the rebels who then formed a schism. On the other hand, it is also held that he was himself expelled by the revolting wing from his own Order and left with about half a dozen adherents, with whose assistance, moral and financial, he continued his Temple.

As their first magical gesture of independence, the rebels changed the name of the Order to The Stella Matutina. Ruled for a year by a committee of twelve, developments forced them to realise that this was far from a satisfactory arrangement. Inasmuch, however, as it had

18

taken several years first to brew and then to develop into an open gesture of defiance, the spirit which had conceived the rebellion was not thus at a single stroke to be banished. Having elevated the standard of revolt by expelling their former chief, for many a dismal month was the Stella Matutina haunted by that ghost. After almost inconceivable pettiness and dispute, the rebels were at the end persuaded by circumstance to abandon every feature of their reform to return to the original scheme of appointing Three Chiefs to govern and lead them. Even this, later, was abandoned if not officially then in practice, for a virtual autocracy similar to that enjoyed by Mathers was once again instituted, though on a much smaller scale. The revolt had been in vain. Those finally selected and appointed as the Chiefs were Fratres Sub Spe, Finem Respice, and Sacramentum Regis. These three Fratres conducted the Order of the Stella Matutina in harmony for about a year. Then, for various reasons, Sacramentum Regis chose to resign. At the meetings held to appoint his successor, differences of the most trivial character continued to arise. Indeed, the spirit of fraternity and wisdom had departed, leaving its averse antithesis, the venom of destruction, to dwell in their midst. Another split developed. Apparently one wing of the schism, thoroughly alarmed in all its bourgeois incompetence and fear by the recent disturbances to the peace of the Order, attributed that cycle of catastrophe to the occult content of the Order teaching, and because of this were now desirous of casting aside as valueless, from the spiritual point of view, the whole of the magical tradition. Their intention was to retain a sort of indeterminate Mysticism of the type which has so often brought disrepute upon the subject, coming to regard their Temple as an adjunct, a clandestine back-door to the Church in some one of its many forms—with especial attractions, I believe, to the Anglo-Catholic groups. One other and more important group

19

within the schism, led by Fratres Finem Respice and Sub Spe carried on full Temple work, more or less adhering to the original plan of the Golden Dawn routine as laid down in the documents drawn up by MacGregor Mathers.

Thus we find in place of a consolidated fraternity at least three separate groupings of individuals engaged in the practice of the Golden Dawn ceremonial system in open Temple, perpetuating as best they might the traditions of the Magic of Light. There was, first, the diminutive group under the leadership of S.R.M.D., still retaining the original Order name. To him were still loyal the Temple or Temples that a few years prior to the final crash had been instituted in the United States of America. Both F. R. and S. S. were in charge of a Stella Matutina Temple, and it is my belief that after a while even they parted company or conducted separate groups, the one in London calling itself the Amoun Temple, and the latter in Edinburgh, Amen-Ra by name. In London also, a separate Temple was being conducted by Frater Sacramentum Regis calling itself the Reconstructed Rosicrucian Order, a group characterised by its exclusive devotion to Christian Mysticism, its rituals being elaborated into verbose and interminable parades of turgidity.

Formerly united by a single fraternal bond, we now see several Temples, being conducted by different groupings of individuals who, while pretending to fraternal communion, had but little sympathy with and affection for the sister Temples of the schism. The slander that was invented and swiftly circulated, as only malice can be circulated, is unrepeatable. Few individuals of real worth were exempt from this network of scandal which enmeshed the whole organisation. This man was an adulterer, that a dipsomaniac—and even after the lapse of more than thirty years this slander is still current. So thoroughly had the central unity of the Order broken up that each

20

of these Stella Matutina Temples appointed its own Imperator, Cancellarius and Praemonstrator, considering itself by these gestures an autonomous occult body. Thus began the downfall of organised magical instruction through the semi-esoteric channels of the Hermetic Order of the Golden Dawn. Whatever else should be insisted upon in Magic, unity is the prime essential. A united body of manifestation at all costs should have been maintained. And the old adage "United we stand, divided we fall" is no idle phrase, especially since the elimination of the "heresy of separateness" is one of the cardinal injunctions of the Great Work. The separate Temples decided to fall independently of how or why or where the other groups fell. Each was smug, complacent and fully confident that it alone continued the magical tradition. The result is that to-day those original Temples are either dead or moribund. While they may have given rise to yet other groups, there is not one of the latter which is not in a diseased condition.

One can hardly help recalling the bitter admonition given by S.R.M.D. to the organisers of the schism. He said, in effect, and in later years Frater Sub Spe corroborated that statement, that he was the principal Chief of the Order by whom and through whom the Order had originally been organised to disseminate the magical tradition. Remember, he warned, what happened to the Theosophical Society after Blavatsky had departed, and there began the disintegration of the world-wide society she had founded and fed with her own life blood. Certainly Mathers' prophecy seems to have vindicated itself. Just as there are innumerable sects claiming to be the original Theosophical Society and professing allegiance to the principles taught by Blavatsky, so are there now several decaying Temples claiming unbroken descent from the original Isis-Urania. Each insists fervently that it alone is the genuine Order; all others are schismatic and

21

unimportant. To-day, as stated above, not one of these surviving Temples is in an even moderately healthy condition. Nor have they ever been since the early days of their foundation. An amusing sidelight on human nature is disclosed by the fact that in one of the Obligations retained by the schismatic groups, there is still the original clause, "Do you further undertake not to be a stirrer up of strife, of schism, or of opposition to the Chiefs."

It was towards the close of 1898, just prior to the revolt, that Aleister Crowley was introduced to the Order by Frater Volo Noscere, receiving his Neophyte initiation at Mark Mason's Hall. It was clear, soon after he joined, that here was a highly gifted young man, and that in many ways, though unrestrained and undisciplined, his was a powerfully magical personality. From Captain J. F. C. Fuller's rather verbose and flamboyant account in the *Equinox* we gather that Crowley was advanced through the grades of the Order quickly, and assimilated the routine knowledge without the least difficulty. Those grades which were not formally separated by automatic delays, were taken at the rate of one a month, and the succeeding ones at the prescribed intervals of three, seven, and nine months. By the time he had taken his Portal grade, the revolt was in full swing, the wisdom and authority of the Chief being on every side doubted and challenged. It was around this period, too, that Crowley's morals and alleged pernicious conduct offended those who were conducting Temple work in London, and the ruling Adepti of Isis-Urania refused to advance him further They refused to do this in spite of the deliberate warning contained in Mathers' manifesto previously mentioned: "What I discountenance and will check and punish whenever I find it in the Order is the attempt to criticise and interfere with the private life of members of the Order . . . . The private life of a person is a matter between himself or herself and his or her God." Whether Mathers was impressed by the promise of Crowley's personality, or whether he decided upon his next step to show contempt for the ruling Chiefs of Isis-Urania Temple, we do not know. But soon after Crowley was invited to Paris where he received the grade of Adeptus Minor from Mathers in Ahathoor Temple. This act served but to inflame the differences which were now openly separating Mathers from his erstwhile followers, and increased the bitter hatred which the Order members bore and still bear for Crowley.

To Crowley's credit, it must be conceded that when open revolt did flame forth, at least he sided with S.R. M.D., acting as his plenipotentiary in the proposed meetings with the rebels in London. The Adepti, however, unconditionally refused to recognise or have ought to do with Crowley. In his fantastic garb of a Highland chieftain with kilt, dirks and tartan, and his face concealed by a heavy mask, he did assuredly make himself so great a laughing stock on that occasion as to make it difficult for anyone to take him seriously.

The conjunction of two headstrong and egotistical personalities rendered it most probable that sooner or later Crowley and Mathers should quarrel. They did, and each went his separate way. Many and varied again are the fantastic accounts of the reasons for that separation. But no matter what their cause, some three years afterwards events led Crowley to denounce Mathers as one obsessed either by Abramelin demons or by the evil personalities of the then incarcerated Horos couple, and that he himself had been nominated by the Secret Chiefs of the Invisible Order to be the outer head of the visible organisation. In the various numbers of the *Equinox*, the official organ of Crowley's personal reformulation of the Order system under the title of A..A...—which does not signify "Atlantean Adepts" as supposed by some stupid reviewer in the Occult Review—may be found Crowley's more or less garbled version of the Order teaching and ceremonial.

At this juncture, it is needful to contradict denials on the part of certain Order members that Crowley did not obtain full Order teaching. Some of these denials are entirely too vehement and "methinks the lady doth protest too much." First of all, I am fully convinced from a close and prolonged study of all Crowley's literary output that he did obtain his Adeptus Minor grade from Mathers after the London group refused to advance him. Unquestionably this is true. Nevertheless, even if this were not the case, he was the *intime*, so to say, of Fratres Volo Noscere and Yehi Aour, both advanced members of the grade of Adeptus Minor, who coached and trained him so that he benefitted by their knowledge and wide experience. Whatever knowledge these Fratres had received from the Order documents was given to Crowley. There is little, I imagine, that he did not receive of the Order teaching then extant, whatever may have been the means fair or foul by which he obtained that teaching. And while he did not publish it in its entirety, it is possible to perceive from hints scattered here, there, and everywhere, that very little had been kept from him. Any student who has a bird's-eye view of the Order system will recognise traces of every aspect of it in the different volumes of Crowley's literary fecundity.

Had Crowley published the entire body of knowledge, only slightly editing the redundancy and verbose complexity of Mathers' literary style—had he issued that teaching so that it bore some semblance to its original state to indicate what it really was and how practised within the Temple, his exposé might not have been too serious. It is possible that he might have been acknowledged as a benefactor of mankind, even if later on he did ruin his own personal reputation by broadcasting absurd legends and leading a foolishly dissipated life. But it was his special mode of publication which argued against the advisability of partially disclosing the secret knowledge of the Order. He tampered unnecessarily with the Grade rituals, so that their beauty as well as practical worth was gone. It became impossible to form any estimation of the efficacy or construction of those ceremonies from their mutilated shadows in the *Equinox*. Perhaps his aim was to eliminate important parts of the rites and practical work so that interested people, realising that more information was required, would communicate with him for further guidance, thus enabling him to consolidate his position as a leader, and formulate an active Order. This is certainly true of the instruction, for example, on Geomancy. The rituals and teaching were badly mauled, rearranged out of all recognition to their former state, and then surrounded by Yoga instructions, short stories, articles on sex-Magic, poetry—much of it of a dubious nature—and a host of miscellaneous odds and ends.

With Crowley's instructions in the art of Yoga, printed both within and without the *Equinox*, there can be no quarrel. They are amongst the clearest ever produced on the subject and amongst the finest examples of the excellent prose of which Crowley was capable. We, the occult-reading public, are immeasurably the richer for their appearance. Epigrams, short stories, card-games, and libels on former friends, however, can hardly be considered fit companions for occult teaching. It is my confirmed belief that it is practically impossible, without more precise guidance or tuition, to ascertain from the *Equinox* and Crowley's other literary productions exactly what is the actual nature of Magic as a definite practical scheme. His form of presentation, and the other contents of the *Equinox*, created nothing but confusion.

Though a revelation of the inner teaching of the Golden Dawn would have been a boon to mankind, yet manifestly Crowley's manner of presentation ruined the effort. If

25

the breaking of a sacred obligation is at all justifiable—as occasionally it is—it is so only when the matter covered by that oath is revealed in a dignified manner and with a noble spirit, as well as in a style fitting to its intrinsic nature. In such an event, the oath is neither betrayed nor profaned, for in being abrogated on behalf of mankind, the author becomes duly qualified to speak for those with whom alone is the power to bind or loose.

It is not my wish to retract what nearly three years ago I enthusiastically wrote in *The Tree of Life*. It was then my conviction as it is now that there was much of a highly important nature in what this extraordinary man of genius has written and published. But I am also profoundly impressed by this fact. Unless one has first studied Magic from a more comprehensible and reliable source, most of what he has written, albeit based upon his own practical experience, will be in the main unintelligible. Any student who has gained a sympathetic understanding of the Golden Dawn teaching will be capable of discriminating between the futile reprehensible portions of Crowley's work, and of deciding which part of it is a worth-while addition to an already magnificent system. And it is because Crowley concedes to his own credit in his, in many respects, admirable volume entitled *Magick* that he has done Magic inestimable service by reason of his development of it, that I have considered it imperative, together with a number of other reasons of equal urgency, to place the Golden Dawn system before the public. Crowley's claims are, in my estimation, wholly exaggerated. I am far from being convinced that the scheme of theory and practice presented in his literature—extraordinary though it is in many ways, considering that it is a development of the simple basic Golden Dawn material—is equal in any way to the system put into documentary form by S. L. MacGregor Mathers and his colleagues.

26

CHAPTER TWO

SCANDAL

Probably the first piece of publicity given to the Order occurred in connection with the Horos scandal of 1901. It must have been about the beginning of 1910 that it gained further publicity of an equally lurid kind. It was in the spring of 1909 that Crowley began to issue his periodical the *Equinox*, his plan being to issue every March and September one large volume containing in abridged and edited form the rituals and magical instructions. Volume Three, according to an advance notice, was scheduled to contain the Ceremony of the Grade of Adeptus Minor, the most important as well as the most beautiful of the grade rituals employed by the Golden Dawn. As might reasonably have been expected, Mathers learned of this proposal. No doubt Crowley wrote him to that effect. Had Mathers ignored the matter, very few people would have learned anything of the Hermetic Order of the Golden Dawn or, for that matter, of the *Equinox*. But in order to prevent the open dissemination of the Rituals he had written, Mathers immediately instigated legal proceedings, an action which gave a vast amount of unwise publicity to Crowley and the Golden Dawn and to Magic. The hearing promptly came before the Court, thus delaying the appearance of the third volume of the *Equinox*. Evidently, the Court was sympathetic to the case of Mathers, for an injunction was granted. An appeal was lodged at once, and with a display of wit and dry humour, the Court of Appeal set aside the injunction, permitting the immediate distribution of the *Equinox*. The result was that in most of the daily newspapers were long sensational articles on the recent case and on so-called Rosicrucian teaching. Some also reproduced a number of the diagrams used in the grade ceremonies. Even the design painted on the lid of the Pastos or Tomb of Christian Rosenkreutz achieved a certain degree of notoriety. Naturally this did nothing to enhance the already shaky reputation of the Order, though it did produce a measure of publicity on behalf of Crowley.

Crowley was not the only initiate who had decided to write openly concerning the teaching of the Order. W. B. Yeats has written several provocative and interesting essays on the magical system of the Order referring to it by name in his autobiography. In his book *Things Near and Far*, Arthur Machen also speaks of the Order, though somewhat facetiously, as the Twilight Star. Several other individuals had left the Order from time to time, and made use of its philosophy and practical system by instituting cliques and moribund groups of their own.

About four or five years ago, there appeared an anonymous book *Light-Bearers of Darkness*, written by one who claimed to be a former Ruling Chief of the Mother Temple of the Stella Matutina. In this work, which was issued by a woman, everything was done to slander to the utmost the magical system she had never really understood. She had three principal misconceptions. The first was that the Golden Dawn as well as other secret societies were merely channels for nefarious political propaganda. In the main, this is quite baseless. The second was that the teaching of the Golden Dawn emphasised a species of sex-magic or sublimation of sex-forces; this also is inaccurate. Finally, it was alleged that the Golden Dawn, Freemasonry, and many another body were in the hands of an international body of Jewish financiers seeking world domination. This latter is simply a repetition or adaptation of the fraudulent "Protocols of the Elders of Zion."

The facts as they were communicated to me are these. This anonymous author had been left in charge of a London Temple by Frater Finem Respice who had migrated either during or shortly after the War to one of the Dominions. For one thing, her progress in the Order had been entirely too hasty. In order to enable her to reach the exalted degree of Adeptship necessary to govern a Temple she had been rushed through the grades prior to a proper assimilation and understanding of the Order system. Secondly, she had fallen into the usual trap that is set for the unwary, the credulous psychic, of whom there were many in the Order. She announced in due course that she had achieved communication with a Master whose teachings, never previously made known to the world, were about to be given through her. It is unnecessary to dilate on the unfortunate though inevitable debacle that followed. The story is not uncommon. Sadly disillusioned and spiritually bankrupt, the poor woman bitterly attacked the Order which had trained or had attempted to train her. One of her remarks dealing with a certain technique is a revelation of her psychology: "At first the visions are vague and slight, but grow in clarity and seeming reality as the adept develops, until suddenly one day, from apparently nowhere, a mysterious brown-habited monk or brother, a guardian of the Order, a Master, or even a false Christ appears and takes charge of the astral expedition, carrying the Adept away perhaps to some isolated monastery . . . ." If this does occur, and the adept, so-called, is deceived by these astral mirages he has no one to blame but himself, for the Order bestows upon him a highly intricate and reliable technique for testing visions and eliminating what is not desired or required. Should deception take place, the Order methods can hardly be blamed. The credulity and vanity of the seer are responsible. In supposing that she was of such a high rank in spiritual capacity as to be worthy of receiving the attentions of a Master, the author of this book has set up a monument exposing her own fatuity and vanity. The Master naturally turned out to be false, and the swollen bubble of her imagination and pride burst, as such usually do.

As to her claim that the Golden Dawn taught sublimation or other employment of sex-forces, little need be said. That claim is utterly without foundation for the subject of sex is nowhere dealt with, whatever may be the definition of magical forces adopted by the individual student. The psychologist has one explanation, the mystic another; and by neither of them has the last word been said on the subject. The publication of the routine of the Golden Dawn system presented herein—the teaching itself may appear *in toto* during the next few months—· should destroy once and for all the smirch cast upon not so much the Order itself as the fair name of a noble and stately philosophy. That piece of slander has come to my hearing from several sources. How it originated is beyond me, since there is not a single authoritative sentence to substantiate it. All that can definitely be stated here is that I have seen most of the important documents issued to the Zelator Adeptus Minor, including a few of those used by the Theorious Adeptus Minor, and there is nothing in them which could even remotely be interpreted as sex-magic. There is, I am very well aware, a distinct and well-formulated branch of the magical tradition which does concern sex-magic, the sublimation of spiritual force lest it otherwise degenerate into purely libidinous energy. Whether it is a legitimate form of magical practice considered from the highest point of view is not for me here to discuss. There is a German Rosicrucian organisation named the Ordo Templis Orientis, reformulated on the ruins of some older orders by Karl Kellner in the last century, which does possess such a body of teaching focussed about a secret technique, comparable in some ways to the tantric sexual practices. But whether or not my personal feeling is sympathetic to such a system, it must be emphasized that there was no such instruction on this subject in the Golden Dawn.

And I reiterate this denial strongly, despite the fact that Dion Fortune in her article *Ceremonial Magic Un-*

veiled in the Occult Review of January 1933 narrates that
G. H. Soror Vestigia Nulla Retrorsum, Mrs. MacGregor
Mathers, nearly expelled her from the Order for writing
The Esoteric Philosophy of Love and Marriage. Dion
Fortune remarks "It was pointed out to her (Mrs. Mathers) that I had not then got the degree in which that
teaching was given, and I was pardoned." Obviously
this implies or suggests that there was a grade in which
this subject was taught. In a later volume I propose re-
producing the actual ceremonies of initiation, the knowledge lectures, and the instruction documents for practical
Magical work which accompanied progress through the
grades. There is nothing in any of the outer grades
from Neophyte to the Portal degree which bears the least
resemblance to any teaching, esoteric or otherwise, on
love or marriage or sex. And it must require a strangely
constituted mind to read this subject into any of the Zelator Adeptus Minor work.

So far as concerns the other attack—that Jews are in
control of the Golden Dawn and other occult bodies, perhaps the writer is well qualified to answer if not on behalf of Freemasonry, of which he knows little, certainly
on behalf of the Golden Dawn. In a word, the allegation
is preposterous. No Jews are at the head of the Golden
Dawn or ever were. In fact, there are or were very few
Jews in it or any other occult society as members. With
reference to the particular Temple of which the present
writer was once a member, he was the only Jew there.
The number of Jews to-day interested in *any* form of
mystical endeavour is pitifully small.

What may lie at the root of this attack, however, is
the fact that the Golden Dawn employes to a very great
extent, the Qabalah, a mystical system nurtured, though
not necessarily invented, by a few Jewish Rabbis during
the Middle Ages. Though it achieved a wide notoriety,
it never succeeded in becoming popular amongst the vast

body of the Jewish people. Hence it can hardly be called Jewish in any ordinary sense of the word. It is in use within the adytum of the Order because tradition and experience prove it to be an amazingly practicable system, its schema accords with mystical and psychic experience, and moreover it provides an acceptable esoteric interpretation to both books of the Bible. All members of the Golden Dawn were obliged after receiving the Neophyte initiation to learn the Hebrew Alphabet, and a great deal of trouble was taken to teach them to draw the letters accurately. They were also required to learn to write the names of the Sephiroth, Archangels, and Angels in that language. The History lecture makes the statement that "through the Hebrew Qabalah indeed, Europe became possessed of more of the ancient wisdom than from any other source, for it must be borne in mind that the Hebrews were taught at one time by the Egyptians, and at a later date by the Chaldee Sages of Babylon." So much, then, for the legend of Jewish domination.

This book *Light-Bearers of Darkness* must therefore be disposed of as containing nothing at all that explains satisfactorily the Golden Dawn or its magical system. On the contrary, it is a pernicious and nauseating work.

It is now necessary to transfer our attention to the Temples formed in the United States of America. So far, the history of the Golden Dawn is not particularly pleasant reading, though I feel impelled to register an unvarnished account of its sad vicissitudes. Yet events in the United States were even more ludicrous, and the government of the Temples in that country seems to have been conducted in a manner which is less commendable and far more grotesque and ridiculous than ever it had been in England.

The principal facts, as far as I can discover, concerned with the American Temples are said to be these. A certain Mrs. Lockwood who is alleged to have been at

32

one time an associate of William Quan Judge, the American Theosophist, received from S.R.M.D., the honorary degree of Adeptus Exemptus, and by her was the first American Temple founded—either in Chicago or Philadelphia, calling itself the Thoth-Hermes Temple. For some years this Temple languished, unperturbed by the devastating blows being dealt at the unity of the European groups. It attracted to itself a small but serious body of occult students. Eventually, the inevitable quarrels broke up its simplicity. These led to the withdrawal of Mr. and Mrs. Lockwood, the Imperator and Praemonstrator respectively, of that Temple. The Editor of an American occult journal, Michael Whitty by name, was appointed Praemonstrator, his sister became the Imperator, and a certain well-known astrologer became Cancellarius. These events took place about 1918. I am obliged to use the ordinary names of these people since their Order mottos were never communicated to me.

Prior to his death in 1917, Mathers had formed a sort of concordat with Frater Sub Spe who had been conducting a Scottish Temple—which was known as the Order of the A. O. Mathers, his wife, and Frater S.S. worked more or less in harmony. Upon the decease of Mathers, Soror Vestigia in collaboration with Sub Spe took over the Order affairs, and handled matters even more unintelligently than had Mathers himself before. Various other quarrels broke out in Thoth-Hermes and the other American Temples, and the manner in which Vestigia handled these quarrels and disagreements caused a great deal of dissatisfaction on every hand. Everybody doubted her ability and integrity and leadership.

Moreover, she was responsible for publicity of a kind which seems so incredible that were it not well authenticated beyond all doubt, one would be inclined to dismiss it as another of the altogether fabulous exaggerations grown up around the Golden Dawn. It has been stressed here that the Order preferred to mask itself with a shroud of secrecy and mystery. No mention of its existence to the outside world was encouraged, and nobody outside the recognised circle of initiates was supposed to know aught of its occult nature, or the character of its spiritual technique. Speaking of the question as to whether he himself knew anything of the so-called unwritten Qabalah, Mathers publicly refused to admit either that he did or did not. This attitude he recorded in his introduction to the *Qabalah Unveiled* published at the time of the commencement of the Order. In a later edition, issued about 1926, Mrs. Mathers contributed a foreword which stated in no uncertain words that her late husband *had* known of the unwritten Qabalah. Not only so but that he had been one of the principals involved in the foundation of an occult school, as to the nature of which her disquisitions concerning the philosophical principles underlying the symbolism of the Lily and the Rose and the Cross left no trace of doubt. This was not all. The evidence is that she caused to be printed for American distribution a pamphlet which claimed a Rosicrucian status and origin for the Order. So far as the Golden Dawn in the Outer is concerned this is baseless from no matter what point of view. It is only the Second or Inner Order of the R.R. et A.C. which may consider itself as Rosicrucian. This grotesque pamphlet, nevertheless, was distributed widely. Following upon this, she gave encouragement to a Frater in Chicago to initiate into the Order anybody who was possessed of the sum of ten dollars. The result was that very soon the country was flooded with Neophytes who, without ever having seen the interior of a Temple, had received some sort of 'initiation' by post. Rightly so, this exasperated and exhausted the patience of those whose very souls were concerned with the proper maintenance of the Order. A number of them thereupon severed their relations with the Temple, with

Vestigia and her group, and two or three of them formed Orders and Temples of their own, teaching Tarot and various aspects of the Qabalah. How many of these latter are living and which are moribund cannot be said. The whole situation there became .utterly chaotic. The same lack of unity and true occult procedure which had previously manifested itself in England assumed far more outrageous proportions in the United States.

Dion Fortune is another who has made innumerable public references to the Golden Dawn. Glibly, she refers to its teachings as the Western Esoteric Tradition. Whether her various expositions tally with the official teaching contained in the actual Order documents must be left to the individual reader to determine for himself when once those documents are made public. In many ways I hold much respect for and sympathy with this clever writer, though this must not prevent my criticising her attitude to the Order system, an attitude which I hold to be in parts quite erroneous and not in accordance with fact.* Her principal piece of work to which my attention herein will be directed is her article *Ceremonial Magic Unveiled.* In that very forthright article, certainly she gave utterance to many things which bear the sign of truth, among them being an apprehension that "the veil of the Temple of the Mysteries is being drawn back at the present moment . . . . So far as I can see,

*Since the above was written (January 1935) I am happy to announce that Dion Fortune has vindicated herself from the unfortunate stigma with which she branded herself in the works I have cited. She has issued through Messrs. Williams & Norgate, a book entitled *The Mystical Qabalah,* which is an extraordinarily lucid and learned exposition of certain ideas fundamental to the Order philosophy. In future years, this book must undoubtedly be considered a masterpiece in its own sphere. Happily, it is free of most of the misconceptions which elsewhere have been propagated, though the presence of several erroneous statements which could have been obviated by reference to or quotation from the Order documents indicate as few things can the necessity of publishing these documents so that individual readers might form their own interpretations.

ceremonial Magic is coming out into the open . . . . For any organisation to try and close the sluice gates against it by oaths of secrecy, is to keep back the Atlantic with a broom."

The time, I think, has now come for the Veil to be drawn back that the golden Sun of the hidden knowledge may irradiate its glory not only upon obligated initiates but upon students of psychology and occultism wherever they may be. And I agree that for the pontiffs of the Order to attempt to prevent that disclosure would be a reactionary gesture which would entail their utter destruction. In fact, the whole position has become both ludicrous and intolerable. Disaster and corruption have long been trailing in the wake of the Golden Dawn, shadowing it since the date of its English inception, and at long last overtaking it. Since the entire system is conducted contrary to the best interests of Magic, dire necessity is the cause of this present introduction to its system, and the proposed future exposition of its scheme of training which antedates its Order mode of transmission.

As already said, Dion Fortune is a pungent writer, with a facile pen and, after a certain manner, a keen analytic sense. Had she accepted no reservations, she could have written a highly presentable account of Order teaching. She has produced several books and a vast amount of journalism. Yet in spite of all this, she has done no more than throw out an occasional hint, accompanied by the merest fragment of Order teaching, simply mentioning that she is in possession of the teaching of the so-called Western Esoteric Tradition. She has restrained her pen, it is quite evident, not out of respect for the obligations nor because the Order in her estimation was anything but moribund. Neither has she felt that the time was unripe for a public presentation of its doctrines, for frequently she has expressed herself verbally as well as in writing as believing that the veil of the Temple must

36

be drawn. Having, however, founded a fraternity of her own, it may be that she did not feel that the public presentation of esoteric knowledge would assist the growth of her group. While she may be doing a great service to that society, the question suggests itself, "Is that withholding of vital information beneficial to the wide-spread occult-reading public?" It seems a pity to me that these veiled and guarded references to the Order system should continually be made in public as though to offer a tempting sugar-plum to prospective members, as a bait to join another fraternity, without producing a definite exposition of that system. It is too simple a matter, alas, for misconceptions to arise and tenaciously be held. If any writer had issued a book which promulgated misinformation about the mission of Madame Blavatsky and the teaching she recorded, one would imagine that no time would be lost by the Theosophical bodies in responding to the challenge by publishing verifiable facts which, while not widely known, were already accessible to those who wished to have them. Yet when there are disseminated doctrines not rooted in veridical magical tradition, and attacks published on the goodwill of the Order, one would have thought that responsible Order members would have considered it unwise and impolitic, for the sake of humanity itself, to let those assumptions go unquestioned. A simple statement of fundamental principles should have been issued. Such would have been invaluable for a variety of reasons. There has been entirely too much complacency within the Order and not sufficient anxiety to keep unsullied the name and character of its traditions. Assuredly the members are prevented by solemn obligations from publicly discussing the Order or its teaching. So much the worse, then, for both the teaching and the Order. If memory serves me aright, one or two anonymous articles of a very petty nature, issued from a so-called authoritative source, were published in the *Occult Review* answering

Dion Fortune's article, but they amounted to absolutely nothing. Their tenor was of the same small-minded obscurantist spirit which has dogged the Golden Dawn from the beginning.

Obligations were originally intended to protect the esoteric tradition rather than the Order. It is not the Order as an organised body which is important but the order system, its magical teaching, and its time-honoured methods of spiritual development. There have been in the past many Orders of varying degrees of efficiency. There has been but one body of doctrine which has been handed down by countless generations of unselfish devotees. In the future necessity may arise for other Orders; their teaching will be the age-old Magic. It is this ancient Wisdom-Religion which is of the utmost value and importance to the welfare of mankind, and it is this traditional science of the soul which should be preserved and protected from every sort of corruption, and from every possibility of misconception.

An Order is simply a temporary vehicle of transmission —a means whereby suitable individuals may be trained to awaken within their hearts the consciousness of the boundless Light. But sooner or later, it would appear that the initiates foster loyalty to the external husk, the shell, the organisation of grades at the expense of that dynamic spirit for which the shell was constructed. So often has it happened in the past. Every religion stands as eloquent witness to this fact. It is the fate which has overtaken the Golden Dawn. Practically the whole membership is fanatically attached to individuals conducting Temple work as well as to the mechanical system of grades of the Order. But when this piece of teaching and that document of importance is withdrawn from circulation, mutilated, and in some cases destroyed, none has come forward to register an objection.

Its Chiefs have developed the tyranny of sacerdotalism.

They have a perverse inclination towards priestcraft, and secrecy has ever been the forcing ground in which such corruption may prosper. Obligations to personal allegiance whether tacit or avowed, is the ideal method of enhancing the personal reputation of those who for many years have sat resolutely and persistently upon the pastos of the hidden knowledge. If by any chance the hidden knowledge were removed from their custody, their power would be gone. For in most cases their dominion does not consist in the gravitational attraction of spiritual attainment or even ordinary erudition. Their power is vested solely in the one fact, that they happen to be in possession of the private documents for distribution to those to whom they personally wish to bestow a favour as a mark of their esteem.

Perhaps it may be possible to summarise the essential character of the Golden Dawn as an organisation, quite apart from its teaching, in the significant phrase *fin de siécle*. Having been founded just prior to the nineties, using the latter word to denote a special period in recent social history, it incorporated within itself all the inherent faults and vices of that period. The fact that it admitted numerous theatrical people to the ranks of its membership indicates the presence of superficiality and self-satisfaction. There was also a strong provincial element of crudity and stolidity. And many of its senior members, including MacGregor Mathers himself, were incurable *poseur*. There is one rumour of a certain Soror F. who donned her full Adept regalia for the purpose of attending a fancy dress ball. And many others, too, connived to acquire a budious notoriety. So completely were these characteristics the hall-mark of the period that once having found their place in the external structure of the Order it was later found impossible to eradicate them, even after the lapse of these many years. The only lasting solution is for the Order deliberately to sink into utter abeyance for about ten years. Then, with a new and younger membership, captained by decent honest folk at the helm, reformulate itself on a much more solid foundation minus the Victorian frills and ruffles which were so thoroughly the curse of its forebears. The Chiefs and the initiates of the past, as well as of the present day, forgot that grades and glorious titles were no indications at all of spiritual attainment, no criteria of interior enlightenment. High grades and complimentary titles such as "Greatly Honoured Chief", "Very Honoured Hierophant" and "Adeptus Minor" which were always in circulation, while useful in assisting the culture of a high standard of good manners, remind one of a certain Qabalistic expression "External splendour but interior corruption." Fine feathers do not make fine birds.

In a letter sent to the writer just over two years ago by one of the Chiefs of a certain Temple, one in the priest-craft and obscurantist tradition, there occurs this sentence inspired by the publication of my *Tree of Life*: "May be I am wrong, but I take the view that reticence on these subjects is still necessary and I deplore the revelation of much that is accurate in what you have given out, while fearing still more the possible results of what you have said that is inaccurate and sometimes dangerous." The Chief, I fear me, is wrong. The sole reason, now that I have acquired some experience of the Golden Dawn, that suggests itself to me for deploring the revelation of its magical system—and of course it is a weighty one with those whose temperament it is to domineer—is that for purposes of prestige and love of power a secret is a most invaluable weapon. Especially so when loyalty and devotion is poured by the rank and file of the membership into the organisation itself, thus vitalising and increasing the power of the priest. While I am not in the least concerned in this place to defend the above mentioned book, it may be left to the individual reader to discover how much of its *essential* body was doctrinally inaccurate by comparing it with the printed documents appearing in my forthcoming volume *The Golden Dawn*.

With reference to the Order teaching, Dion Fortune justly remarks, and here at least I am in complete accord with her, "There is no legitimate reason that I have ever been able to see for keeping these things secret. If they have any value as an aid to spiritual development, and I for one believe that they have the highest value, there can be no justification for with-holding them from the world."

Because I believe this teaching may help if only a small portion of mankind, I resent this half-unveiling of the Temple. The bitter memories of my own search for the hidden wisdom force me to regard as useless mere references in passing to Magic in place of a well-formulated exposition. Magic is more important than the Order in exactly the same way as the original Theosophy is infinitely of greater value than any Theosophical organisation which has espoused its cause. Since the Order is decadent on any scale of values, it is essential that the whole system should be publicly exhibited so that it may not be lost to mankind. For it is the heritage of every man and woman—their spiritual birthright.

In the darker periods of human history when no occult school dared show its head because of persecution, there were the Custodians of this ancient tradition who cherished its mysteries in their hearts and embodied its precepts and technique within the depths of their own being. And there will always be such. But no longer do they exist within the Order of the Golden Dawn or the Stella Matutina. Secrecy was originally instituted for fear of tyrannical oppression from state and church, and also to prevent the possibility of abuse by ignorant people. Modern progress has eliminated the likelihood of persecution. Ridicule, arising from spiritual darkness, has taken its place, a much more potent and devastating weapon—though from another standpoint, and so far as I am concerned, a perfect safeguard. The powerful mechanical inventions of different kinds which are already known and employed by mankind at large renders it extremely improbable that the secret wisdom is likely to receive more abuse without the pale of the Order than it has already received from within. Anyway, the wide-spread extraversion of humanity enhances the hidden knowledge with a degree of protection which at no time did it enjoy by means of the convention of secrecy and silence.

From a psychological point of view alone, the effect of with-holding a secret from the possible fertilising influence of the outside world is, if the process be prolonged too indefinitely, one of corruption and sterility. No less an authority than Dr. Jung of Zürich corroborates this viewpoint in his *Modern Man in Search of a Soul.* He declares that "anything that is concealed is a secret. The maintenance of secrets acts like a psychic poison which alienates their possessor from the community." It is perfectly obvious, well within every-day experience, that in small doses a poison may act as a precious and priceless remedy. As an example of this, we have the preservation of secret teachings in the Mystery Cults of antiquity—stabilising and civilising influences on the people of their times. Yet, on the other hand, it is also evident that the slightest abuse of so dangerous a poison entails corruption, and disaster is bound to follow in its wake. Those same Mystery Cults of by-gone eras stand as eloquent examples of this theorum. "It resembles a burden of guilt which cuts off the unfortunate possessor from communion with his fellow beings."

How true is this of the Golden Dawn? Particularly where the unconscious sense of guilt was heightened by the fact that its secrets were secret no longer. Because of its dumb inability to extend the inspiration of its system to the outside world, it was incapable of sharing in the communal life of the people about it. And Jung observes significantly that if, however, we are fully conscious of the nature of what is concealed the harm is considerably less than otherwise might be the case. As I shall labour at some length to prove, there was no clear recognition of what was the true nature of the Golden Dawn secret teaching. With the result that very few individuals attempted to carry out in their own personal spheres the entire scheme of training which would justify the further retention of that teaching. Once the deteriorating influence which accompanies the guarding of such knowledge had been faced, and its membership then acted accordingly, the effect of the Golden Dawn upon its own and subsequent generations, as well as upon civilisation as a whole could have been enormous. I believe it could have amounted to a leavening of the soul of modern man. An instilling of regenerating factors into the Unconscious of the race. So insidiously, however, had that poison acted upon it, that because of wilful blindness, its more recent Hierophants became unable efficiently to initiate newly admitted candidates. How could they initiate? First of all, they had flatly refused out of fear to include within their own spiritual training those processes which aim at the impacting of magical forces upon the material plane. Ceremonies of initiation were, naturally, quite frequently celebrated. But the essential and dynamic illumination which is the outcome of inspired initiation was wholly absent. Thus no cultural or beneficial influence was allowed to percolate to the outside world through its Neophytes and other members.

That the initiations were not effective is, I believe, self-evident. Like vaccination, initiation becomes apparent when it has properly "taken." The primary and direct effect of a successful initiation—or the real progress through the grades, which progress consists in the gradual bringing into operation of the higher Genius, the real Self—is the stimulation or production of creativity, some form or other of genius. Indeed it is manifest without further argument that the present rank and file of the Golden Dawn, perhaps through no fault of its own, is utterly sterile. The tendency of the organisation itself to schism and disintegration is self-evident of its prolonged barrenness, since it has persistently denied itself the opportunity of fertilisation from without and even from the intrinsic inspiration of its own magical rites. The system and technique of spiritual training which it affords to initiates unquestionably could have been a mighty cultural and integrating factor in the enhancement of the race consciousness. The whole mass of people could have been automatically exalted to a higher level of integration and spiritual awareness by a more insistent and wider application of its technique for the development of spiritual and artistic genius. Instead, the history I have narrated indicates colossal failure and sad futility. Whatever cultural influence the Order did exert upon the surrounding people exhausted itself soon after the opening of this century.

Despite the truth of these facts, some may feel that the history of the Order is such an unhappy one, that it need never have been brought into the open light. To this, the only response must be that it has not been exactly an enjoyable task to disentangle these facts. My motives have been to prove without a doubt that no longer is the Order the ideal medium for the transmission of Magic, and that since there have already been several partial and irresponsible disclosures of the Order teaching, a more adequate presentation of that system is urgently called for. It is to provide that presentation which is the cause of my present writing. Only thus may the wide-spread misconceptions as to Magic be removed. Again, referring to this corruption and the unhappy history of the Order, it must be realised that so long as any disease is unrealised and unrecognised, its scourge cannot be checked, nor can any adequate course of treatment be prescribed. With a frank recognition of the existence of that disease then efforts can be made in the direction of therapy. Light is often said to be a perfect therapeutic agent. Therefore I here disclose this tainted history to the healing light of day, that the tradition of the divine Theurgy may be cleansed from the foul psychic associations of the past twenty or thirty years that once more it may take its rightful place as an integral and inspiring part of modern life and culture—which in the right hands undeniably it may be.

Some also may believe that this history, so far from being pretty, shows also that Magic itself is of the same nature, and that it would have been better to let the Order destroy itself together with the system which it espoused. But my view is that the vicissitudes of the Hermetic Order of the Golden Dawn as an exoteric organisation cast not the least doubtful reflection on Magic. If it be assumed that those from whom this viewpoint may emanate will be, let us say, devout Christians or Theosophists of an orthodox leaning, these I can only remind of the numberless ghosts asleep under their own roofs. The distinction between Christianity and the organisation of the Church has been defined too frequently to warrant repetition here. And for the Theosophy taught by Madame Blavatsky I have the greatest admiration, considering myself a staunch adherent to the general terms of the philosophy which she so ably expounded. But the events which coincided with her high office in the Theosophical Society, to make but little mention of the unhappy incidents which occurred immediately following her death, might lead the outsider to suppose that because the Theosophical Society failed, so did Theosophy fail. With the logic of this statement I cannot agree, for

45

nothing could be further from what is true. Theosophists will perhaps agree with my attitude in this connection, arguing that the Society failed because of its refusal to apply practically the lofty precepts of Theosophy. Therefore I retain most strongly the view that an identical attitude must be held as to the facts of Magic in connection with the Golden Dawn. It was the latter that failed. It was the body of membership which failed to rise to the high spiritual standard set up by Magic. To lower the standard or the ideal of attainment in order that a greater number of small-minded people might not feel their vanity wounded would be a crime than which few could be greater.

Possibly many will still consider me evil or irresponsible in venturing to break solemn obligations, by making public items of knowledge I had sworn to keep secret. However, for many years the obligations have been regarded even within the Order as formalities, obsolete conventions, and little more. Most of the clauses, with the sole exception of that dealing with the actual with-holding of knowledge from the outside world, have already been broken again and again, if not in the letter then certainly in their spirit.

The historical data reproduced above stand as ample evidence to that end. It would be a simple matter to produce a half-a-dozen members from different Temples who would corroborate the accuracy of this testimony. A straightforward presentation of magical knowledge to remove it from the custody of incompetent and unworthy guardians is thus very necessary. It does not matter to me or to mankind from what source the revelation comes, or by whom it is made. But what is important is this. The time has arrived when the petty barriers withholding important and invaluable knowledge from sincere students must be broken down. In any event, those barriers have been rendered pretty flimsy and ineffectual because of the events occurring within the last thirty-five or forty years, and it would be childish to maintain any longer that they continue to be effective barriers. Several efforts have been made to publish these facts, though most have been inadequate and badly conceived. Their very inadequacy *demands* that a fuller and more explicit presentation be made. Individuals there may be who will retort that the failure of these past efforts indicates that the time is not yet ripe for such a disclosure, and that reticence in these matters is still as necessary as it always was. I deny this. More probably the truer facts are that vanity and ordinary human weakness and egotism are the fundamental causes which have hitherto baulked the efforts of former writers on the divine Theurgy. These also are the same failings which within the Order have been so responsible for such a strict adherence to the letter of the Oaths in lieu of the inner spirit.

In point of fact, however, these views have long been officially held, and I can assure the reader that I am not being particularly original in giving utterance to them. On several occasions, when conversing with my former Chief about the necessity for a wider circulation of Occult knowledge, she herself admitted that in the future it must reach a greater number of people than heretofore. She even gave expression to the heretical view that Crowley may, as he claimed, though not necessarily in the way whereof he boasted, have been guided in his decision to publish Order teaching. Naturally, this was a theme too painful to discuss at greater length, and she never explained that view further since the name of Crowley was anathema.

Another incident that should be recorded as significant evidence will also show that this action of mine may not be so unspeakable as may seem at first sight to some of the occult obscurantists. Last year, (1934) the privilege was mine of introducing an eminent psychologist to the

Order. Upon receiving the preliminary paper with the simple statement that an obligation to complete secrecy as to the teaching of the Order was necessary, he cavilled rather. He thereupon put it to me that he was bound by his Hippocrates oath as a physician "to be willing to teach all I know to those who may be willing to learn it . . . . I come to the Order knowing something and wishing to know more. That which I know already I am prepared to teach; but I understand that that which I learn from the Order I am not allowed to teach . . . . I feel that I can only join if I am free to carry out the terms of the Hippocratic oath which I presume to be that antecedent moral law which the Order would be prepared to respect in my case."

Personally, of course, I was thoroughly in sympathy with his viewpoint. As a formality, however, I communicated his letter to the Temple authorities for an official answer. The reply to the psychologist comprised the opinion that the Order Obligations referred principally to two matters. First, the name and address of the Temple must not be divulged. Nor, secondly, were names of the members to be disclosed. And the Chief went on to say, he could make use of whatever portions of the teaching he saw fit to pass on to such of his patients as were capable of receiving it.

If this be the case, and there is documentary evidence to prove it, then my present labour receives official sanction. It is far from my intention to reveal the names or whereabouts of the Temples. That is not a matter of importance to me, and I am not willing to engage in petty acts of spite or hatred. Nor do I intend to disclose the names or extent of the membership. These are genuine secrets and shall be respected. I do not seek to embarrass any individual holding a prominent position by stating his association with a body which is regarded with suspicion and contempt. Whoso can profit by the teachings of the Order is another matter, and such ought to have them without being obliged to pay the exorbitant price of undue humiliations and oppression.

Quite apart from this official sanction, there is an even more important reason which demands that the teaching be removed from the hands of its present incompetent guardians. With each of the schisms and quarrels which have occurred from time to time, various official documents have been lost, or, what is simply criminal, deliberately destroyed. Unbelievable though it may sound, the attitude seems to have been, "If I can't make use of these papers, then nobody shall. Into the fire they go." When one of the Chiefs of a North country Temple died many years ago, it is alleged that his widow promptly seized all his Order manuscripts and, so we are told, destroyed them. Very much the same sort of thing has occurred in other of the Temples. This lamentable behaviour has been confined to no particular group. Where there have been students in the Order this insane attitude has always manifested itself. There is, so I am told, an individual in charge of one of the Temples whose understanding of certain magical matters is not too profound. Rather than acknowledge this, which would have been forced upon him were documents on these subjects distributed, and then questions asked, it is alleged that he has preferred not to circulate them. From personal knowledge, it would not be difficult to prognosticate similar withdrawals and wholesale conflagrations occurring in other of the Temples within the not far distant future.

It is to prevent this wastage of invaluable psychological material and this criminal destruction that impels me to make public the salient aspects of that system. It would be monstrous and tragic were this knowledge lost to those who seek the Light along this Path. Yet, if this knowledge is not soon transferred into a more permanent form than private manuscripts whose distribution is a

49

matter of whim and caprice, the passage of not many more years may see its utter disappearance from our midst. Corruption is rife within the Temple. The rank odour of decay poisons the air, while the heavy dust of slow disintegration accumulates over its furniture, befouling the minds of its members. Very soon, no Temple of the Hermetic Order of the Golden Dawn or the Stella Matutina may survive. Their documents will have been deliberately consigned to the flame. Those members who, having previously resigned or demitted, do possess a complete set of the documents, think only in the petty terms of starting another little cult or sect, while nowhere does anyone show either the courage or the least concern for mankind to contemplate the publication of the entire truth. The commencing anew of another private group has led inevitably to the same ignominious and fatuous end. For while there is aught to retain as a secret, giving certain egotistical personalities domination over somewhat weaker aspirants, so long will the abuses remain. So long also as the present absurd examination system continues its drunken course and members are flattered by inane titles and grades, there can be little hope of healthy magical organisation.

Perhaps the degeneration of the Order has been inevitable. There is a great deal of misapprehension both within and without the sanctuary as to the true purpose of the magical system. Whatever abuses may legitimately be ascribed to Aleister Crowley, at least he did have the acumen and keen insight to see, as well as to record on occasion in black and white, the true goal of all theurgic training. But even he and evidently many another have strayed from the clearly defined path of the great work in quest of Masters. Many a year has been wasted in that goalless journey. Many a valuable soul lost meandering in that wilderness of deception and delusion. If Masters there be, then they come and go as they will, selecting their own disciples in the light of their own individual needs and in accordance with their own peculiar standards. Although in the Neophyte Obligation there is a reference to the "divine guardians of this Order who live in the light of their perfect justice and before whom my soul now stands," and while also in the Adeptus Minor Ceremony there is mention made of the ancient Fratres of the Order or the Three Chiefs, to converse with whom meetings are often held in the Vault, that quest for Masters is nowhere officially recognised or approved by the Order system. There is no single clause in any of the several obligations which stresses the search for a Master, astral or physical, as the key note of the Great Work. On the contrary, it is strongly inculcated throughout, both by direct statement as well as by implication, that the Great Work and the goal of the eternal quest is the discovery of Adonai, union with the higher and divine Genius, the knowledge and conversation of the Holy Guardian Angel. The central Tiphareth clause of the grade of Adeptus Minor has as its avowed intention, with the whole of that exceedingly fine ceremony, the exaltation of the candidate's consciousness to the divine.

But it is abundantly clear that more energy has been expended in vision and other kinds of groups, within and without the Vault, under the auspices of those in authority, than ever has gone into the higher spiritual or magical invocations. In fact not much encouragement was ever given to the latter.

While it is true that the central task of training is the attainment of the knowledge and glory of the higher Self, a good deal of preparatory discipline is necessary in order to prepare the lower self, to render it a fit and worthy vehicle of the Light. For different individuals at different times these preparations must naturally vary, and the Order system takes cognisance of these differences. The early elemental grades strengthen the fundamental basis of the soul, that it may be firmly established to receive the

51

influx from on high. After the Adeptus Minor grade has been taken, then the development of spiritual insight and the consecration ceremonies and magical operations set forth in the Order formulae further prepare and strengthen every phase of the mind, which is thus trained to be the immediate vehicle through which the Light may manifest. These ceremonies of consecration and invocation give power and stability to the soul, moulding it into a well-trained instrument of the higher and divine genius. All this is legitimate magic, and if sustained leads to legitimate ends; although again I emphasise that no official encouragement in these latter days were given to these legitimate pursuits. In fact, magical initiative was definitely discouraged—as well I know. But whether or not magical initiative was encouraged, clairvoyant seances for contacting Masters have but little place in a true magical curriculum. In any event, such groups devoted to no matter what end are contrary to the true intent of the Order training which deliberately demands of the aspirant that he will labour at the prescribed work alone and unassisted. There is no clause in any of the obligations recommending group work of any kind.

It can confidently be asserted that these latter have been amongst the most fruitful causes leading to the disruption of the Order. The beginnings of this type of seance or group work go back to the early years of its establishment in England. It would seem that as far back as 1897 circles were formed in Edinburgh and London as secret societies working within the Order, legalised apparently both by D.D.C.F. and S.A. Some few of the Adepti of that period did have the perspicacity to realise the enormous danger involved therein, and shortly after the revolt we find W. B. Yeats attempting in spite of enormous and obstinate opposition to persuade Soror S.S.D.D., to amalgamate the smaller groups that one central consolidated organisation might be formed. Nor would it have been so serious had these little groups been content to occupy themselves with the work of the curriculum in the straightforward magical technique. But they busied themselves, as did the anonymous author of *Light-Bearers of Darkness,* with matters outside the scope of sensible pursuits—contacting Masters, Arabs, Northmen, shades of deceased Egyptian priests and so forth, and obtaining from them so-called advanced teaching.

That none may accuse me of injustice or prejudice in this connection, may I suggest for one thing a careful consideration of the article by Dion Fortune already referred to. Though her purpose was ostensibly to review a book purporting to outline the general fundamentals of Magic, the whole orientation of that article was in an utterly false direction. The book mentioned contained no single reference to Masters, stressing from the first page to the last that the principal object of the Great Work consisted in the acquisition of a nobler and wider consciousness, which there was termed the Holy Guardian Angel. Significantly enough, however, Dion Fortune ignored this repeated definition. The concluding paragraphs of her article give utterance to the baseless view that Magic and the Golden Dawn system were devoted to "picking up contacts" of the Masters, to use the horrible *clichés* of a neo-occult movement. Yet neither *The Tree of Life* or the Golden Dawn system itself were concerned in any way with Masters or their "contacts."

Round about 1902, a pamphlet entitled *Is the R.R. et A.C. a True Magical Order?* was privately issued by Frater D.E.D.I., former Imperator of Isis-Urania Temple. In this pamphlet he deplored bitterly and attacked precisely this sort of group seance for conversation with astral Masters. The thirty years which have since elapsed have taught very few people the needful lesson. For only about four or five years ago, in one of the Temples which was approaching the end of its tether, several clairvoyants, instead of applying themselves with true magical work to build up a centre of power, began a circle to seek help from astral Masters. Moreover immediately after my initiation into the grade of Adeptus Minor, or rather the day following, the Chief ushered me into the Vault, and there alone we two were visited by the so-called Invisible or Secret Chiefs of the Order. It would be useless repeating any of the chaotic communications received at any of these meetings, despite the fact that I heard a good deal about them. In one way or other my person seems to have been involved in some of them.

In addition, let me register another disagreement with some of those who have written publicly on magical matters. With them, I also disbelieve the descriptions of Masters provided by Leadbeater and others of that ilk, and the claim of MacGregor Mathers that he met three Adepts in the Bois de Boulogne. These are old wives' tales. But on the other hand, and contrary to those views, I would not dare deny the fact that Masters *may* have a physical existence. Undoubtedly there may well be Masters on the Astral. The Blavatskian definition of Nirmanakayas is precisely that. But why seek for teachers in that phantom world of illusion and deception when here, in this physical world, there are those inhabiting bodies of flesh and blood who have attained and achieved? The entire philosophy of Magic and mystical effort demands their physical existence in this world and not in another; and there are authentic voices to that end.

In *Sane Occultism,* we find Dion Fortune claiming that "we find the Master on the inner planes before we are assigned to a teacher on the outer plane." This is very much to be doubted. If by "Master on the inner planes" she refers to the higher Genius, for that sometimes is the implication of the phrase, then no contradiction need be noted. But if that phrase is employed in its conventional occult sense, then I beg leave to differ. There is no authoritative teaching for that statement either from tradition, obtaining within the Order, or issuing from the very few legitimate occultists of the past fifty years. Most of those who have experientially claimed some such astral contact have either come to psychic or spiritual grief, or else through their own words have confounded the truth of such statements. Certainly that extraordinary collection of erudition, wisdom and wide sympathy, *The Mahatma Letters* makes no such claim. For if one thing ever was insisted upon by the Mahatmas of any age and period, it was that they were men, and *not* astral beings. Moreover, there are countless testimonies available to this truth. History, profane and religious, points out to us great beings like Krishna, Buddha, Lao-Tze, Christ, Rosenkreutz, and many another noble character, living their lives among men. Those mentioned have indeed passed on either to their well-deserved rest, or to other kinds of work, whether here or elsewhere we cannot definitely say. But their type, their successors, disciples and descendants, these are still with us and amongst us, not necessarily confining their activities to Tibet, India, or Egypt, or any other especial country. They are the finest flower of the growth of mankind to be found wherever and whenever mankind labours with all its might towards a spiritual ideal. And it is, I suggest, the augmentation of their ranks which is the final *raison d'etre* of the Order of the Golden Dawn.

CHAPTER THREE

LIGHT

Occasionally one comes across an unintelligent critic of the Order who complains that its ceremonial system is garbled and incoherent, or that its fundamental elements have long since been available in books. For the most part this complaint is, I think, nonsense. Whatever else may be said of the Order and its scheme of instruction, at least this is true. It taught the true term of Mysticism and the art of Ceremonial Magic as few other systems have, not even excepting the Eastern schools. For confirmation of this statement, consult as an example any mediaeval or even recently published text-book on Magic. From this, make an attempt to construct a workable ceremony for, let us say, the consecration of a Flashing Tablet—a ceremony which at once will be coherent, effectual and not offensive to the inner sense. The consecration ceremonies used within the Golden Dawn for the charging of implements, though simple in nature, are perfect and classical examples of the Ceremonial Art which it would be difficult if not impossible to better. Few improvements could be suggested for these rituals. Whoever was responsible for them matters not in any way. Whether or no it was MacGregor Mathers who wrote them, or Fräulein Sprengel or her Masters and Teachers, we have very much to be grateful for. If as some suggest, Mathers was merely a scribe in the employment of Dr. Westcott, a scribe employed to expand the rubric of the mythical cipher manuscripts no matter what their mysterious origin. And we must not neglect to record our debt to Westcott who discovered them, and Mathers who transcribed their cipher.

The complaint of incoherency and plagiarism is therefore of little importance. It is as absurd as the other point of view widely within the Order that none of the Order teaching may be found in exoteric published sources. There *are* some who consider the whole system esoteric in all its aspects.

Certainly some of the parts of the Golden Dawn rituals may be discovered in different ancient and mediaeval books on Magic. This has never been denied by any of its more informed members who have an eye to research. Some of its isolated parts undoubtedly derive from both Henry Cornelius Agrippa and the Abbot Trithemius. Dr. John Dee, the *Sepher Yetzirah*, the *Fama Fraternatitas*, and the works of Franz Hartmann are other writers and works which have been responsible for many contributions to the system. Several passages in the Grade Rituals are taken verbatim from the books of the Bible, the Chaldaean Oracles, the Zohar, and scholars no doubt will recognise many another source.

But what the Order and its scribes have performed is a much subtler thing. They have synthesised into a coherent whole this vast body of disconnected and widely scattered material, and have given it form and meaning. All these separate items of knowledge garnered from innumerable sources have been wielded into a practicable and effectual system, which surely cannot be said for example of Levi's *Transcendental Magic* or, in fact, any other book extant, ancient or modern. It was no mean task, no light accomplishment, to have gathered these many passages and techniques and coordinated them as we now have them. The substance of the system may already have appeared in quite a number of books—and it is to our advantage that we do employ a system which has its powerful roots in tradition; we gain immeasurably by the use of a traditional mode of working. But the coordination, the synthetic nature of the entire scheme, the effectual soul of the Rituals, as it were, these have their foundation in sources which have never previously found their way into any written work. Without a doubt they are the fruit of innumerable adepts and true initiators, the result of whose verified and tested experience has been handed down to us from countless generations.

One of the most important backgrounds of the system, the fundamental philosophy underlying the same, is the scheme of the Qabalah. An understanding of this mysticism is an absolute necessity if the function of the Rituals is to be understood. For the grades of the Order are referred to the Ten Sephiroth of the Tree of Life, and the passage from one grade to another is accomplished by way of the several connecting paths. Hence a knowledge of the attributions and significance of those Sephiroth and Paths is required if the rituals are to be appreciated in their entirety. The knowledge lectures to be reproduced later give the actual skeletal form of that philosophy, and that skeleton of names, ideas, and symbols should be carefully memorised. Perhaps, in passing, it may be as well to emphasise the fact that symbols are of the utmost importance in the Qabalistic and magical scheme, for it is by their intervention and use that we are able to enter into the life of other parts of our consciousness, and through them into the consciousness of the universe about us. C. G. Jung, the psychologist, aptly remarks that "the unconscious can only be reached and expressed by the symbol . . . . The symbol is, on the one hand, the primitive expression of the unconscious, while on the other hand, it is an idea corresponding to the highest intuition produced by consciousness." Further details of the Qabalah with the principal symbolic ideas that it employs may be found in my *Tree of Life*, and since it is unnecessary to repeat what is there explained at some length the reader must be referred to that book. All that need here be stated are but the basic facts, the barebones as it were, of that philosophy.

Since it is primarily a mystical method, the Qabalah has innumerable points of identity with the more ancient systems elaborated by other peoples in other parts of the world. Its most important concept is that the ultimate source from which this universe, with all things therein, has evolved is *Ain Soph Aour,* Infinite or Limitless Light. This is to be conceived, so far as the human mind is capable of conceiving such abstractions on the metaphysical plane, as an infinite ocean of brilliance wherein all things are held as within a matrix, from which all things were evolved, and it is that divine goal to which all life and all beings eventually must return. Issuing from or within this boundless Light, there manifests the Tree of Life. Qabalists have produced a conventional glyph indicating thereupon ten numerations, or Sephiroth, which are the branches of that Tree growing or evolving within space, ten different modes of the manifestation of its radiation. These finally culminate in the evolution of a material product, the final term of a series of spiritual and ethereal regions, each with its own laws, conditions, and "times" if one may borrow terminology from Dunne's "Experiment with Time." This final term is named *Malkuth,* the material and physical universe. These Sephiroth are not to be construed as ten different portions of objective space, each separated by millions and millions of miles—though of course they must have their correspondences in different parts of space. They are, rather, serial concepts, each condition or state or serial concept enclosing the other. The distinction between them is one of quality and density of substance, as well as representing different type-levels of consciousness, the "lower" worlds or Sephiroth being interpenetrated or held by the "higher." Thus *Kether,* the Crown, is in *Malkuth,* as one axiom puts it, by virtue of the fact that its substance is of an infinitely rare, ubiquitous, and

59

ethereal nature, while *Malkuth,* the physical universe, is enclosed within the all-pervasive spirit which is *Kether* in precisely the same way that Dunne conceives Time No. 1 to be enclosed or contained, or moving as a field of experience, within Serial Time No. 2.

So far as concerns the Boundless Light, the Qabalah teaches that it is an abstract impersonal principle, an exalted condition of consciousness rather than of substance —an essence or spirit which is everywhere, and at all times, expressed in terms of Light. Though wholly impersonal in itself, and without characteristics cognisable to our human minds, *Ain Soph Aour* is, to all intents and purposes, what is commonly thought of as God. In the system of Tibetan Buddhism, the concept analogous to this is the Void, *Sunyata.* The realisation of the Void by means of the processes of Yoga and the technical meditations of the Sangha is, to quote Dr. Evans-Wentz's book *The Tibetan Book of the Dead,* to attain "the unconditioned Dharmakaya or the Divine Body of Truth, the primordial state of uncreatedness, of the Supramundane *Bodhic* All-consciousness—Buddhahood." In man, the Light is represented by a mighty activity within his soul, the intrinsically pure essence of mind, the higher and divine Genius. Though the Golden Dawn rituals persistently use phraseology which implies the belief in a personal God, that usage to my mind is a poetic or dramatic convention. A number of its very fine invocations are addressed to a deity conceived in a highly individualistic and personal manner, yet if the student bears in mind the several Qabalistic definitions these rituals take on added and profound meaning from a purely psychological point of view. That is, they are seen to be technical methods of exalting the individual consciousness until it comes to a complete realisation of the universal essence of mind which ultimately it is.

Now if we examine these rituals and ceremonies care-

60

fully—and it is my sincere and fervent hope that when eventually they do make their appearance they will be read with much care and attention—we shall find that we can epitomise in a single word the essential teaching and ideal of those rituals. If one idea more than any other is persistently stressed from the beginning of one's initiation into this magical system, that idea is in the word *Light*. From the candidate's first reception in the Hall of the Neophytes when the Hierophant adjures him with these words: "Child of Earth, long has thou dwelt in darkness. Quit the Night and seek the Day" to the transfiguration in the Vault ceremony, the whole system has as its sole object the bringing down of the Light. For it is by that Light that the golden banner of the inner life may be exalted; it is in light where lies healing, and the power of growth. Some vague intimation of the power and splendour of that glory is first given to the aspirant in the Neophyte Grade when, rising from his knees at the close of the invocation, the Light is formulated above his head in the symbol of the White Triangle by the union of the magical implements of the three chief officers. By means of the Adeptus Minor ritual, which identifies him with the Chief Adept, he is slain as though by the destructive force of his lower self, and after being symbolically buried, triumphantly rises from the Tomb of Osiris in a glorious resurrection through the descent of the white Light of the Spirit. The intervening grades occupy themselves with the analysis of that Light as it vibrates between the light and the darkness, and with the establishment within the candidate's personal sphere of the rays of the many-coloured rainbow of promise.

"Before all things," commences a phrase in one ritual, "are the chaos, the darkness, and the Gates of the Land of Night." It is in this dark chaotic night so blindly called life, a night in which we struggle, labour and war incessantly for no reasonable end, that we ordinary human

61

beings stumble and proceed about our various tasks. These gates of the far-flung empire of the night indeed refer eloquently to the material bondage which we ourselves have created—a bondage whereby we are tied to our circumstances, to our selves, to trial of every kind, bound to the very things we so despise and hate. It is not until we have clearly realised that we are enmeshed in darkness, an interior darkness, that we can commence to seek for that which shall disperse the night, and call a halt to our continual projection outwards of the blackness which blinds our souls. As in the Buddhist scheme, where the first noble truth is Sorrow, not until we have been brought by life's experience to understand the world as sorrow, can we hope for the cessation of its dread ravage. Only then does the prospect open of breaking the unconscious projection, the ending of which discloses the world and the whole of life in a totally different guise. "One thing only, brothers, do I proclaim," said the Buddha, "now as before. Suffering and deliverance from suffering."

These restricting circumstances and bonds are only the gates of the wilderness. The use of the word "gate" implies a means both of egress and ingress. By these gates we have entered, and by them also may we go out if so we choose, and by doing so enter the brilliance of the rays of the Sun, and perchance greet the golden dawning of the spiritual splendour. For "after the formless the void, and the darkness, then cometh the knowledge of the Light." As intimated above, one first must have realised that one's soul is lost in darkness before a remedy can be sought to that irresponsible *participation mystique*, and aspire to that divine land which is, metaphorically, the place of one's birth. In that land is no darkness, no formlessness, no chaos. It is the place of the Light itself— that Light "which no wind can extinguish, which burns without wick or fuel."

62

Being "brought to the Light" then is a very apposite description of the function of Magic. It is the Great Work. There is no ambiguity in the conception of the Rituals, for it appears throughout the entire work from Neophyte to Adeptus Minor and perhaps beyond. For the Path is a journeying upwards on the ladder to the Crown of the Tree of Life, and every effort made and every step taken brings one a little nearer to the true glory of the Clear Light. In point of fact, the experience of the rising of Light in both vision and waking state is common to mystics of every age and of every people, and it must be an experience of the greatest significance in the treading of the Path because it appears always and everywhere as an unconditioned thing. It is an experience which defies definition, as well in its elementary flashes as in its most advanced transports. No code of thought, philosophy or religion, no logical process can bind or limit it. But always it represents, spiritually, a marked attainment, a liberation from the perplexing turmoil of life and from every psychic complication, and, as Jung expressed it, "thereby frees the inner personality from emotional and imaginary entanglements, creating thus a unity of being which is universally felt as a release." It is the attainment of spiritual puberty, marking a significant stage in growth.

Symptomatic of this stage of interior growth is the utter transformation that comes over what previously appeared to be the "chaos, the darkness, and the Gates of the Land of Night." While man is assumed into godhead, and the divine spirit is brought down into manhood, a new earth and a new heaven make their appearance, and familiar objects take on a divine radiance as though illumined by an internal spiritual light. In his book *Centuries of Meditation*, Thomas Traherne gives an interesting description of the rapture of the inner personality, its reaction to the world when it is freed by the mystical experience from all entanglements. He says: "The corn was

63

orient and immortal wheat, which never should be reap-
ed, nor was ever sown. I thought it had stood from everlasting to everlasting. The dust and the stones of the
street were as precious as gold; the gates were at first
the end of the world. The green trees when I saw them
first through one of the gates, transported and ravished
me, their sweetness and unusual beauty made my heart
to leap, and almost mad with ecstasy, they were such
strange and wonderful things. The men! O what vener-
able and reverend creatures did the aged seem! Immortal
Cherubim! And the young men glittering and sparkling
angels, and maids, strange seraphic pieces of life and
beauty. Boys and girls tumbling in the street, and
playing, were moving jewels . . . . I knew not that they
were born or should die. But all things abided eternally
as they were in their proper places. Eternity was manifest
in the Light of the Day, and something infinite behind
everything appeared . . . ."

And there is another exalted panegyric by Traherne
which I cannot desist from quoting, as it illustrates so
perfectly the magical attitude towards life and the world
when enlightenment has been obtained. For Magic does
not countenance a retreat from life, an escape from the
turmoils of the world; it seeks only to transmute what
was dross into gold, and transform the base and low
into the pure and splendid. "All appeared new and
strange at first, inexpressibly rare and delightful and
beautiful. I was a little stranger which at my entrance
into the world was saluted and surrounded with innumerable joys. My knowledge was Divine; I knew by intuition
those things which since my apostacy I collected again
by the highest reason. My very ignorance was advan-
tageous. I seemed as one brought into the state of in-
nocence. All things were spotless and pure and glorious;
yea, and infinitely mine and joyful and precious. I knew
not that there were any sins, or complaints or laws. I

dreamed not of poverties, contentions, or vices. All tears and quarrels were hidden from my eyes. Everything was at rest, free and immortal. I knew nothing of sickness or death or exaction. In the absence of these I was entertained like an angel with the works of God in their splendour and glory; I saw all in the peace of Eden . . . . All Time was Eternity, and a perpetual Sabbath . . . ."

Such is the stone of the Philosophers, the Quintessence, the Summum Bonum, true wisdom and perfect happiness.

It is to effect this integration, to bring about this psychic release, this exaltation of the consciousness to the Light that the magical system of the Golden Dawn, or of any other legitimate initiating system, owes its existence. The function of every phase of its work, the avowed intention of its principal rituals, and the explicit statement of its teaching, is to assist the candidate by his aspirations to find that unity of being which is the Inner Self, the pure essence of Mind, the Buddha-Nature. Not only does the system imply this by its ritualistic movements and axiomata, but there are clear and unmistakable passages where these ideas are given unequivocal expression. The whole object of Magic and mystical training "is by the intervention of the symbol, ceremonial and sacrament, so to lead the soul that it may be withdrawn from the attraction of matter and delivered from the absorption therein, whereby it walks in somnambulism, knowing not whence it cometh nor whither it goeth." And moreover in the same Ritual, celebrated at the autumnal and vernal equinoxes, the Chief Adept officiating recites an invocation beseeching guidance for the newly-installed Hierophant "that he may well and worthily direct those who have been called from the tribulation of the darkness into the Light of this little kingdom of Thy love. And vouchsafe also, that going forward in love for Thee, through him and with him, they may pass from the Desire of Thy

65

house into the Light of Thy presence." This is succeeded by sentences read by the Second and Third Adepti, "The desire of Thy house hath eaten me up," and "I desire to be dissolved and to be with Thee."

And finally, that not the least vestige of misunderstanding or misconception may remain as to the objects of this divine Theurgy, let me reproduce one last quotation from this same ritual. Referring to the Supernals and the Temple that in old time was built on high, the speech adds, "The holy place was made waste and the Sons of the house of Wisdom were taken away into the captivity of the senses. We have worshipped since then in a house made with hands, receiving a sacramental ministration by a derived light in place of the co-habiting Glory. And yet, amidst signs and symbols the tokens of the Higher presence have never been wanting in our hearts. By the waters of Babylon we have sat down and wept, but we have ever remembered Zion, and that memorial is a witness testifying that we shall yet return with exultation into the house of our Father."

Thus and unmistakably is the true object of the Great Work set before us, and we shall do well ever to keep eye and aspiration firmly fixed thereto. For while the road to the spiritual Zion demands great exertion, and because it is a way that at times proceeds by devious routes, there is great temptation to linger by the roadside, to stroll down pleasant side-lanes, or to play absent-mindedly with toys or staves cut but to assist our forward march. But if we forget not to what noble city the winding path leads us, little danger can overtake any who pursue it steadfast to the end. It is only when the promise of the abiding city is forgotten that the road becomes hard, and the way beset by unseen danger and difficulty.

Prior to attempting a description of a few of the salient points of the Rituals—briefly, for since the latter are soon to make their appearance as a sequel to this book, they must be individually studied and experienced so that an individual point of view may be acquired—it may be advisable to devote a few words to the art of Ceremonial itself.

A useful and significant quotation may be taken from Jung's commentary to Wilhelm's translation of *The Golden Flower,* where there is much that explains the ritualistic functions of Magic. "Magical practices are," is his estimation, "the projections of psychic events which, in cases like these, exert a counter influence on the soul, and act like a kind of enchantment of one's own personality. That is to say, by means of these concrete performances, the attention or better said the interest, is brought back to an inner sacred domain which is the source and goal of the soul. This inner domain contains the unity of life and consciousness which, though once possessed, has been lost and must now be found again."

From one point of view the officers employed in these Rituals represent just such psychic projections. They represent, even as figures in dream do, different aspects of man himself, personifications of abstract psychological principles inhering within the human spirit. Through the admittedly artificial or conventional means of a dramatic projection of these spiritual principles in a well-ordered ceremony a reaction is induced in consciousness. This reaction is calculated to arouse from their dormant condition those hitherto latent faculties represented objectively by the officers. Without the least conscious effort on the part of the aspirant, an involuntary current of sympathy is produced·by this external delineation of spiritual parts which may be sufficient to accomplish the purpose of the ceremony. The aesthetic appeal to the imagination—quite apart from what could be called the intrinsic magical virtue with which one of the G.D. documents deals at some length—stirs to renewed activity the life of the inner do-

main. And the entire action of this type of dramatic initiatory ritual is that the soul may discover itself whirled
in exaltation to the heights, and during that mystical elevation receive the rushing forth of the Light.

Thus, in the preliminary Neophyte or ◎ = $\boxed{0}$ grade,
the Kerux personifies the reasoning faculties. He is the
intelligent part of the mind, functioning in obedience to
the Will; the Qabalistic *Ruach* in a word. The higher
part of that mind, the aspiring, sensitive, and the intuitive
consciousness, the *Neschamah,* is represented by the He-
gemon who ever seeks the rising of the Light, while the
active will of man is signified by the Hiereus, the guardian against evil. The Hierophant, in this initial ceremony
of Neophyte, acts on behalf of the higher spiritual soul
of man himself, that divine self of which but too rarely,
if ever at all, we become aware. "The essence of mind
is intrinsically pure," is a definition of one of the Bodhi-
sattva Sila Sutra, and it is this essential state of enlightenment, this interior self, Osiris glorified through trial
and perfected by suffering, which is represented by the
Hierophant on the dais. He is seated on the throne of the
East in the place of the rising Sun, and with but two or
three exceptions never moves from that station in the
Temple. As the Qabalah teaches, the everlasting abode
of the higher Self is in the Eden of Paradise, the supernal sanctuary which is ever guarded from chaos by the
flaming sword of the Kerubim whirling every way on the
borders of the abyss. From that aloof spiritual stronghold
it gazes down upon its vehicle, the terrestrial man, evolved
for the object of providing it with experience—involved
in neither its struggle or its tribulations, yet, from another point of view, suffering acutely thereby. And seldom does that Genius leave its palace of the stars except
when, voluntarily, the lower self opens itself to the higher
by an act of sincerest aspiration or self-sacrifice, which
alone makes possible the descent of the Light within the

heart and mind. Thus when the Hierophant leaves the throne of the East, he represents that Higher Self in action, and as Osiris he marks the active descent of the supernal splendour. For he utters, while leaving the dais with wand uplifted, "I come in the power of the Light. I come in the Light of Wisdom. I come in the Mercy of the Light. The Light hath healing in its wings." And having brought the Light to the aspirant, he retires to his throne, as though that divine Genius of whom he is the Temple symbol and agent awaited the deliberate willing return of the aspirant himself to the everlasting abode of the Light.

Even in the communication of the usual bourgeois claptrap of secret societies, the signs and grips, all these are explained solely in terms of the quest for the Light. Also the various groupings of officers and their movements in the Temple are not without profound meaning. These should be sought out, since they incessantly reiterate the implicit purpose of the rite. Thus, at the altar, the three principal officers form about the candidate a Triad, representing again the Supernal Clear Light of the Void, and these again are represented by the number of the circumambulations. The white cord bound thrice about the waist has reference to the same set of ideas, the binding of the lower by the higher. Even upon the altar are symbols indicating the rise of Light. A red calvary cross of six squares as symbolic of harmony and equilibrium is placed above a white triangle—the emblem of the Golden Dawn. They form the symbol of the Supernal Sephiroth which are the dynamic life and root of all things, while in man they constitute that triad of spiritual faculties which is the intrinsically pure essence of mind. Hence the triangle is a fitting emblem of the Light. And the placing of the Cross above the Triangle suggests not the domination of the sacred spirit but rather a kind of adjustment, its equilibriation and harmony within the inner heart. Despite the fact that the whole of this intricate symbolism can hardly be realised by the candidate at the time of his initiation, its intrinsic virtue is such that unconsciously as an organised body of suggestion it is perceived and noted and strikes the focal centre.

The five grades that follow have as their object the awakening of the elemental bases of what must develop into the instrument of the higher. Awakened and purified, they may be consecrated to the Great Work that they may become worthy vehicles for the indwelling of the Light. First, however, it is necessary that they be awakened. For psychological truism that it is, until their presence is divined their transmutation cannot be accomplished. In symbolic form and pageantry, the ceremony of each grade calls forth the spirits of a particular element. And as a steel placed in close proximity to a magnet receives some degree of its magnetism, and comparable to the electrical phenomenon of induction, so the presence of power induces power. Contact with the appropriate type of elemental force produces an identical type of reaction within the sphere of the Neophyte, and it is thus that growth and advancement proceeds. The speeches of the officers deal almost exclusively with the knowledge pertaining to that grade and element, while excerpts from certain of the Qabalistic books and the ritual fragments of the Ancient Mysteries do much towards producing an impressive atmosphere.

The element offered for the work of transmutation in the Grade of Zelator is the earthy part of the Candidate. The ritual symbolically admits him to the first rung of that mighty ladder whose heights are lost in the Light above. This first rung is the lowest sphere of the conventional Tree of Life—*Malkuth*, the *Sanctum Regnum*. To it is ascribed the first grade and the element of Earth. Quotations from the *Sepher Yetzirah* comprise a fair portion of this ritual. After the Earth elementals are invoked the Candidate is ceremonially conducted to three stations, the first two being those of evil and the presence divine. At each of these stations the Guardians reject him at the point of the sword. Strongly they urge him in his unprepared state to return whence he came. His third attempt to go forward places him in a balanced position, the path of equilibrium, the Middle Way, where he is received. And a way is cleared for him by the Hierophant, who again represents the celestial soul of things. During his journey along the path, the stability of earth is established within him, that eventually it may prove an enduring temple of the Holy Spirit.

The criticism of this and the subsequent elemental grades by Crowley was a little harsh and severe. He rejected them entirely. And in a letter sent to me from a former Praemonstrator of another Temple, these rituals too were condemned in that they were said to be simply a parade, redundant and verbose, of the occult knowledge that S.R.M.D. possessed at that time. In one sense, of course, what both those critics claim is perfectly true. The principal formulae and teaching are concealed in the preliminary Neophyte Grade and that of Adeptus Minor, and it is the development of the ideas in these ceremonies which constitutes the Great Work—the uncovering of the essence of mind, the invocation of the higher and divine Genius. These, however, are the high ends and the final goals of the mystic term. Notwithstanding his limitations these are the ultimates to which every man must work. Meanwhile, in order to render that attainment possible in its fullest sense, several important matters require attention. The personality must be harmonised. Every element therein demands equilibriation so that illumination ensuing from magical work may not give rise to fanaticism and pathology instead of Adeptship and integrity. Balance is required for the accomplishment of the Great Work. "Equilibrium is the basis of the soul."

Therefore the four grades of Earth, Air, Water and Fire plant the seeds of the microcosmic pentagram, and above them is placed in the portal ceremony the Crown of the Spirit, the quintessence, added so that the elemental vehemence may be tempered, and that all may work together in balanced disposition. These grades are therefore an important and integral part of the work of initiation, despite short-sighted hostile criticism. To compare them, however, with those which precede and follow, is symptomatic of an intellectual confusion of function. It is rather as if one said that milk is more virtuous than Friday—which, naturally, is absurd. Yet similar comparisons in magical and mystical matters constantly are made without exciting ridicule. Different categories may not be so compared. The purpose of the Neophyte ritual is quite distinct from that of Zelator, and it is mistaken policy to compare them. What rightly could be asked is whether the Zelator and the other elemental grades accomplish what they purport to do. That is another matter. The concensus of experienced opinion is on the whole that they do. Whether the history of the Golden Dawn proves them to be anything other than cheap psychic stimulants, as yet other critics claim, is again a matter which is not for me to decide.

The candidate, by these grades, is prepared it is argued to enter the immeasurable region, to begin to analyse and comprehend the nature of the Light which has been vouchsafed him. The first three elemental grades could be taken just as quickly as the candidate, at the discretion of the Chiefs, desired. There were no requirements other than indicating by examination that the appropriate meditations had been performed and items of knowledge comitted to memory.

The grade after the Earth ceremony is that of Theoricus. It is referred to the Ninth Sephirah on the Tree of Life, *Yesod* the Foundation, and to it are attributed the sphere of the operation of Luna and the element Air. Here the candidate is conducted to the stations of the four Kerubim, the Angelic choir of Yesod. The Kerubim, the holy animals of Ezekiel's vision, are defined by MacGregor Mathers in his *Qabalah Unveiled* as the presidents of the elemental forces, the vivified powers of the letters of Tetragrammaton operating in and through the four elements. Each element is, by this system of attributions, ruled by a Kerub under the aegis of one of the letters of YHVH. It is always through the power and authority and zodiacal symbol of the Kerub that the elemental spirits and their rulers are invoked. In this ritual, as in all the others, important formulae of practical magic are concealed.

At this juncture of the ceremony with the Airy elements vibrating about and through him, the Zelator is urged to be "prompt and active as the Sylphs, but avoid frivolity and caprice. Be energetic and strong as the Salamanders, but avoid irritability and ferocity. Be flexible and attentive to images, like the Undines, but avoid idleness and changeability. Be laborious and patient like the Gnomes, but avoid grossness and avarice. So shalt thou gradually develop the powers of thy soul, and fit thyself to command the spirits of the elements."

In each grade, several drawings and diagrams are exhibited, each one conveying useful knowledge and information required in the upward quest. The Tarot Keys are also dealt with, as indicating the stages of that journey and depicting the story of the soul. It may not be possible because of the exigencies of space to reproduce a pack of Tarot cards based upon esoteric descriptions—though I should very much like to do so. But by using the Waite and the available Italian packs, and by comparing them with the accounts given in the rituals, the imagination of the reader will render this omission unimportant.

The third grade is that of Practicus referred to the

73

Sephirah *Hod*, the Splendour, the lowest of the Sephiroth on the left hand side of the Tree, the Pillar of Severity. Its attributions refer to the sphere of the operation of the planet Mercury, but more especially to the element of Water which is invoked to power and presence. As I have previously remarked, and it bears constant reiteration, the Tree of Life and the Qabalistic scheme as a whole should be carefully studied so that the aptness of the attributions to both the Sephiroth and the Paths may be fully appreciated. Two Paths lead to the Sphere of Splendour—the Path of Fire from Malkuth, and the reflection of the Sphere of the Sun from Yesod. Water is germinative and maternal whilst the Fire is paternal and fructifying, and from their interior stimulation and union is the higher life born, even as has been said, "Except ye be baptised with water and the Spirit ye cannot enter the Kingdom of Heaven."

Therefore in this grade the Candidate is led to the Sphere of stagnant water, which by the presence of solar and fiery elements is vitalised and rendered a perfect creative base. Some of the speeches in the ritual are depicted as issuing from the Kabiri, the Samothracian deluge Gods, though the main body of the ritual consists of the sonorous and resonant versicles of the *Chaldaean Oracles*—the translation, I believe, of Dr. Westcott. Briefly, the entire symbolism of the Practicus grade is summarised by the position on the altar of the principal Golden Dawn emblems so arranged that "the cross above the Triangle represents the power of the spirit rising above the triangle of the Waters." That also indicates the immediate task ahead of the Candidate. At this juncture, too, the diagrams displayed begin to take on especial significance, and though their theme apparently is biblical in nature, accompanied by explanations in a curious phraseology consonant therewith, they are nevertheless highly suggestive, as containing the elements of a profound psychology. After this grade follows an automatic wait of three months, referred to the regimen of the elements, a period as it were of silent incubation, during which time the rituals are given to the candidate that he may make copies for his own private use and study.

Were it advisable it would be a most happy task to devote several pages of this book to praising the excellence of the four Elemental Prayers. The reader will notice that each one of the elemental ceremonies closes with a long prayer or invocation which issues, as it were, from the elements themselves. The Prayer of the Salamanders, one of the most eloquent of the four, may be seen in *Comte de Gabalis,* while the Air invocation or Prayer of the Sylphs can be seen both in my *Tree of Life* and Eliphas Levi's *Transcendental Magic.* These should be silently read, continuously meditated upon and frequently heard fully to be appreciated, after which the reader will find his own personal reactions crystallising. Recited by the Hierophant at the end of the ceremony, these prayers voice the inherent aspiration of the creatures of the elements towards the goal that they are striving in their own way to reach, for here they are conceived as blind dumb forces both within and without the personal sphere of man. They are given assistance by the human beings who, having invoked them and used their power, strive to repay in some measure the debt owed to these other struggling lives.

The fourth grade of Philosophus carries the candidate one step further. The Sephirah involved is *Netzach,* Victory, to which is referred the operation of the planet Venus and the element of Fire, while the paths that connect to the lower rungs of the ladder are principally of a watery nature. Thus the elements encountered are of an identical nature with those of the preceding grade. But here their order and power is quite reversed. Previously the Water was predominant. Now the Fire rages and

75

whirls in lurid storm, with Water only as the complementary element whereon it may manifest, and in order that due equilibrium may be maintained. These two are the primary terrestrial elements which intelligently controlled and creatively employed may lead eventually to the restoration of the Golden Age. And by their transmutation a new paradise may be re-created from the darkness and chaos into which formerly it had fallen. For the Light may not legitimately be called forth upon man nor dwell within him, until chaos has been turned into equilibrium of complete realisation and enlightenment. And until order has been restored to the lower elements of his earthy kingdom, neither peace nor inner security may be his rightful lot.

The symbols depicted while traversing the Path of Peh, the reciprocal path which joins the spheres of Fire and Water, indicate the results as it were of the first stages of the Path, for the Tarot card shown demonstrates the destruction of a Tower. The three holes blasted in the walls symbolise the establishment of the divine through and following the destruction of the false conceptions and complacency of the outer self. Though Fire and Water, warmth and moisture, are essentially creative, their stimulation within the being of the Neophyte draws his attention perhaps for the first time to the chaotic condition of his natural existence, and the complete psychic muddle into which his ignorance and spiritual impotence have stranded him. Evocative of the highest within his soul, these elements equally call forth that which is base and low. The first step is analytical, the levelling down of all that man formerly held true and holy—the chaos, the darkness, and the Gates of the Land of Night. An unhappy state, but a very necessary one if progress is to be made and if the chaos is to be transcended. From these ruins may be erected the new temple of Light, for it is always from the rubbish heap that are selected the materials for the manifestation of god-head. These symbols have a dual application. Not only do they refer to the epochs of creative evolution whose memory has long since faded even from the visible memory of Nature, but also to the recapitulations of those periods within personal progress on the Path. And it is in connection with those recapitulations that the "aspirant on the threshold of Initiation" observes Crowley, "finds himself assailed by the 'complexes' which have corrupted him, their externalisation excruciating him, and his agonised reluctance to their elimination plunging him into such ordeals that he seems (both to himself and to others) to have turned from a noble and upright man into an unutterable scoundrel." These are the experiences and events which occur to every aspirant when initiation forces the realisation upon him that "all is sorrow." In fact, the criterion or hall-mark of successful initiation is the occurrence of these or similar experiences. The whole universe, under the stimulation of the magical elements and inward analysis, seems to tumble like a pack of cards crazily about one's feet. This is the *solvé* half of the alchemical *solvé et coagula* formula. Analysis must precede synthesis; corruption is the primitive base from which the pure gold of the spirit is drawn. So far as the nature of the environment and the creative power of the personal self permits, the task implied by the *coagula* formula is to assemble them and remould them nearer to the heart's desire.

In two Altar diagrams—one called the Garden of Eden shown in the Practicus Grade, and the other called The Fall, shown in the Philosophus Grade, all these ideas are expanded and synthesised. They should be carefully studied and receive long meditation, for in them are many clues to the spiritual and psychological problems which beset the traveller on the Path, and they resume the entire philosophy of Magic. Many hints, moreover, which may be found useful as assisting meditation are contained in *The 'Curse' from a Philosophical Point of View* in the second volume of Blavatsky's *Secret Doctrine* in connection with the Prometheus myth and the awakening of Manas, mind.

Since it is my intention to reproduce both of these diagrams at a later date, very little by way of explanation need now be said. The first depicts a personified representation of the three fundamental principles in Man. Each of these is apparently separate, functioning independently on its own plane without cooperation with, because unaware of, either the higher or the lower. Principally, it represents man in the now departed morning of the race, in the primary rounds of evolutionary effort when not yet had self-consciousness been awakened or won by self-induced and self-devised efforts, and when peace and harmony prevailed both within and without by right of heritage rather than through personal labour. The diagram appears in the Water grade of Practicus, since Water is a fitting representation of this placid peace. At the summit of the diagram stands the Apocalyptic woman clothed with the Sun of glory, crowned with the twelve stars, and the moon lying at her feet. Her symbolism pertains to the supernal essence of mind, representing thus the type and symbol of the glittering Augoeides, the *Neschamah.* "It is," remarks Jung, describing an analogous conception in *The Golden Flower,* "a line or principle of life that strives after superhuman, shining heights." At the base of the tree stands Eve, the *Nephesch,* who, in opposition to this divine Genius, stands for the "dark, earth-born, feminine principle with its emotionality and instinctiveness reaching far back into the depths of time, and into the roots of physiological continuity." Between the two stands Adam, supported by the fundamental strength of Eve, the *Ruach* or Ego not yet awakened to a realisation of its innate power and possibility. From the larger point of view

78

he represents the race as a whole and is "the personified symbol of the collective Logos, the 'Host', and of the Lords of Wisdom or the Heavenly Man, who incarnated in humanity." Otherwise he represents the individual candidate on the Path just prior to the awakening of the "sleeping dogs" within his being.

Beneath these three figures sleeps a coiled many-headed dragon, silent, unawakened, still. None it would seem is aware of that latent power, titanic and promethean, coiled beneath, the active magical power centred in man, the libido, neutral, neither good nor evil in itself.

Very similar in some respects to the foregoing is the diagram revealed in the Philosophus grade. As the peace of Eden was shown during the Water grade, so in the Grade of Philosophus the power of Fire is shown to have called forth catastrophe. Formerly coiled beneath the tree, the hydra-headed Dragon in this Diagram has usurped its proper place, and its several horned heads wind their way up into the very structure of the Tree of Life, even unto *Daath*. Lured downwards by the tree of knowledge (and we may remember in what sense the Bible speaks of the verb "to know") towards the "darkly splendid world wherein continually lieth a faithless depth," Eve, the lower self, ceases to give support to Adam; she has yielded to the awful fascination of the awakening psyche. Far easier is it to fall than to climb to the distant heights. Yet the Fall is catastrophic only from one viewpoint. The awareness of the rise of the Dragon endows man also with consciousness of power—and power is life and progress. The Dragon is the symbol of the enemy to be overcome, as well as, when eventually conquered, the great prize to be won at the end.

The Qabalistic Sephira of *Daath* is the conjunction of Chokmah and Binah on the Tree of Life, the child of Wisdom and Understanding—knowledge. It refers to the symbolic sphere formed within or above the *Ruach* by means of experience, and this assimilated becomes transmuted into intuition or faculty of mind. But fundamentally it is the ascent of the Dragon, or, if you wish, the obsession of the personality by a welling up of the unconscious archetypes, which first renders *Daath* a possibility; it is the Fall which is responsible for the acquisition of self-knowledge. Thus "it stands proven," claims Blavatsky "that Satan, or the Red *Fiery* Dragon, the 'Lord of Phosphorus', and *Lucifer,* or 'Light-bearer', is in us; it is our mind—our temper and Redeemer, our intelligent liberator and saviour from pure animalism." In the evolutionary scheme the Fall occurs through a higher type of intelligence coming into close contact with nascent humanity, thus stimulating the psyche of the race—or so the magical tradition has it. The recapitulation of this epoch within the individual sphere of consciousness proceeds through the technique of initiation whereby the Red Dragon is stirred into activity through contact with the fructifying powers of the elements. The use of the divine prerogative brought about by the magic of experience, the awakening of *Daath,* brings disaster at first, because the awakened psyche is imperfectly understood and so abused for personal ends. But that very disaster and that abuse confers the consciousness of self. Consequently, the realisation of sorrow as it impinges on the personality and an understanding of its causes must inevitably constitute the first impetus to perform the Great Work, even as it comprises the motive first to seek the services of the analytical psychologist. This impetus and this self-consciousness are the prime implications of *Daath.* Its signification is a higher type of consciousness, the beginning of a spiritual rebirth. It acts as a self-evolved link between the higher Self on the one hand at peace in its Supernal Eden, and the human soul on the other, bound by its fall to the world of illusion and sense and matter. But until that self-consciousness and acquired knowledge are turned to noble and altruistic ends, sorrow and suffering are the inevitable results. Continually will the Red Dragon, the inverted power of the eros, ravish the little kingdom of self until such time as we lift ourselves up to the diviner parts of our human nature, thus conquering the foe by driving it back to its proper realm, using but neither ignoring nor repressing experience and its fruit to transcend our own personal limitations.

Let me quote a few especially appropriate lines from Jung in connection with this Fall, when the fundamental basis of the *Ruach* has been attracted to the kingdom of shells, and when Malkuth has been completely cut off from the other Sephiroth: "Consciousness thus torn from its roots and no longer able to appeal to the authority of the primordial images, possesses a Promethean freedom, it is true, but it also partakes of the nature of a godless *hybris*. It soars above the earth, even above mankind, but the danger of capsizing is there, not for every individual to be sure, but collectively for the weak members of such a society, who again Promethean-like, are bound by the unconscious to the Caucasus." It will not do, then, for the Adept to be cut off from his roots, but he must unite and integrate his entire Tree, and train and develop the titanic forces of the unconscious so that they become as a powerful but docile beast whereon he may ride.

The Adeptus Minor grade continues the theme of these two diagrams. Escorted into the Vault, the Aspirant is shown the lid of the Tomb of Osiris, the Pastos wherein is buried our Father Christian Rosenkreutz, and on that lid is a painting which brings fulfilment to the narrative of the preceding diagrams. It is divided into two sections. The lower half of the painting depicts a figure of Adam, similar to his presentation in the Practicus grade, though here the heads of the Dragon are falling back from the Tree, showing the Justified One, the illuminated adept, by his immolation and self-sacrifice rescuing the fallen kingdom of his natural self from the clutches of an outraged eros. But above this, as though to show the true nature behind the deceptive appearance of things, is illustrated a noble figure of majesty and divinity, described in the Ritual in these words. "And being turned I saw seven golden light-bearers, and in the midst of the Light-bearers, one like unto the Ben Adam, clothed with a garment down to the feet, and girt with a golden girdle. His head and his hair were white as snow, and his eyes as flaming fire; his feet like unto fine brass as if they burned in a furnace. And his voice like the sound of many waters. And he had in his right hand seven stars, and out of his mouth went the Sword of Flame, and his countenance was as the Sun in his strength."

It is to effect this redemption of the personality, to regenerate and transmute the enormous power of the Red Dragon, and attempt to bring the individual to some realisation of his potential godhead, that is the object of the Adeptus Minor ceremony. It is for this reason that I hold that the Golden Dawn or magical technique is of supreme and inestimable importance to mankind at large. In it the work of academic psychology may find a logical conclusion, so that it may develop further its own particular contribution to modern life and culture. For the system indicates the psychological solution of the *animo* problem. "Arise! Shine! For thy light is come!"

Between the grades of Philosophus and Portal, an interval was prescribed of seven months, the regimen of the planets. During that period, devised to assist the silent fructification of the seeds planted within, a review was advised of all the preceding studies. Such a review was, of course, imperative. As D.D.C.F. wrote: "Remember that there is hardly a circumstance in the rituals even of the First Order which has not its special meaning and application, and which does not conceal a potent magical formula. These ceremonies have brought thee into contact with certain forces which thou hast now to learn to awaken in thyself, and to this end, read, study and re-read that which thou hast already received. Be not sure even after the lapse of much time that thou hast fully discovered all that is to be learned from these. And to be of use unto thee, this must be the work of thine own inner self, thine own and not the work of another for thee, so that thou mayest gradually attain to the knowledge of the Divine Ones."

The Grade of the Portal, which conferred upon the candidate the title of Lord of the Paths of the Portal of the Vault of the Adepti, is not referred to a Sephirah as such. It may, however, be considered as an outer court to Tipharath, exactly as the Adeptus Minor ceremony may be considered Tiphareth within. Its technical attri-bution is the element of Akasa, Spirit or Ether. Referred to the Veil *Paroketh* which separates the First and Second Orders, it is intermediate between the elemental grades and that of Adeptus Minor. A crown to the four lower elements, this Rite formulates above Earth, Air, Water and Fire the uppermost point of the Pentagram, reveal-ing the administration of the Light over and through the kingdom of the natural world. It concerns itself with a recapitulation of the former grades, co-ordinating and equilibriating the elemental self which, symbolically sac-rificed upon the mystical altar, is offered to the service of the higher Genius. In that grade, too, aspiration to the divine is strongly stressed as the faculty by which the veil of the inner sanctuary may be rent. It is the way to realisation. The five Paths leading from the grades of the First to the Second Orders are symbolically traversed, and their symbols impressed within the sphere of sensa-tion.

A gestation period of at least nine months had to elapse prior to initiation to the grade of Adeptus Minor, and since there can be no possible misunderstanding of

83

the purpose and nature of this beautiful ceremony it requires not the least comment from my pen. It explains itself in one of the speeches: "Buried with that Light in a mystical death, rising again in a mystical resurrection, cleansed and purified through him our Master, o brother of the Cross of the Rose. Like him, o Adepts of all ages, have ye toiled, like him have ye suffered tribulation. Poverty, torture, and death have ye passed through. They have been but the purification of the gold. In the alembic of thine heart, through the athanor of affliction, seek thou the true stone of the wise."

Since frequent reference has been made to the Vault of the Adepti, just a few words of description may not be amiss. As a climax to the very simple Temple furniture of the Outer grades, it comes as a psychological spasm and as a highly significant symbol. The Vault itself is a small seven-sided chamber set up in the centre of the Temple. Each side represents one of the seven planets with their manifold correspondences. The mediaeval Rosicrucian manifesto *The Fama Fraternatitas,* translated in Arthur Edward Waite's *Real History of the Rosicrucians,* describes it at great length, though I shall quote briefly as follows: "We opened the door, and there appeared to our sight a vault of seven sides and seven corners, every side five foot broad and the height of eight foot. Although the sun never shined in this vault, nevertheless it was enlightened with another Sun, which had learned this from the sun, and was situated in the upper part of the centre of the ceiling. In the midst, instead of a tomb-stone, was a round altar . . . . Now, as we had not yet seen the dead body of our careful and wise Father, we therefore removed the altar aside; then we lifted up a strong plate of brass, and found a fair and worthy body, whole and unconsumed . . . ."

Around this fundamental symbolism, the Golden Dawn synthetic genius had built a most awe-inspiring superstructure. The usual Order symbolism of Light was represented by the white triangle and Rose placed upon the ceiling, whilst the floor design was so painted as to represent the Red Dragon and the forces of the primitive archetypes upon which the candidate trod down as emblematic of his conquest. Placed in the centre of the Vault was the Pastos of the mediaeval founder of the Order, Christian Rosenkreutz—though the pastos is also referred to as the Tomb of Osiris the Justified One. Both of these beings are the type and symbol of the higher and divine Genius. Immediately above this coffin rested the circular altar mentioned in the *Fama*. It bore paintings of the Kerubic emblems, and upon these were placed the four elemental weapons and a cross, the symbol of resurrection. At one point in the Ceremony, the Hierophant, or Chief Adept as he is called in this ritual, is interred in the Pastos, as though to represent the aspirant's higher Self which is confined to the personality which wanders blindly, lost in the dark wilderness. The whole concatenation of symbols is an elaborate and dramatic portrayal of the central theme of the Great Work. In a few words, it depicts the spiritual rebirth or redemption of the candidate, his resurrection from the dark tomb of mortality through the power of the holy spirit.

The psychologist no doubt will see in the Vault a highly interesting and complex symbol of the Mother. Traces of this symbolism may be recognised in the fragments we inherit from the mystery Cults of antiquity. It would be possible and quite legitimate to interpret the Vault in its entirety as referring to the Isis of Nature, the great and powerful mother of mankind, and an analysis of the separate parts of the Vault—the Venus door, the Pastos, the two Pillars—would subscribe to that view. For regeneration and the second birth have always as psychological states been associated with the Mother. And it may be recalled that the *Neschamah* or that principle of man which constantly strives for the superhuman shining heights, is always portrayed as a feminine principle, passive, intuitive, and alluring.

The reader is earnestly recommended to study this Ritual again and again until almost it becomes a part of his very life, incorporated into the fabric of his being, for therein are concealed many highly important and significant formulae of mystical aspiration as well as of practical magic. In it is exemplified the technical "Dying God" formula, about which in *The Golden Bough* Frazer has written so learnedly. Examples of this are to be found in every mythology and every mystical religion that our world has ever known. For we are clearly taught that we are, in essence, gods of great power and spirituality; that we died to the land of our birth in the Garden of Hesperides, and mystically dying descended into hell. And moreover, the ritual demonstrates that like Osiris, Christ, and Mithra, and many another type of god-man, we too may rise from the tomb and become aware of our true divine natures. The principal clause of the lengthy Obligation assumed during that ceremony is the key to the entire grade. "I further solemnly promise and swear that, with the Divine permission, I will from this day forward apply myself unto the Great Work, which is so to purify and exalt my spiritual nature that with the Divine Aid I may at length attain to be more than human, and thus gradually raise and unite myself to my higher and divine Genius, and that in this event, I will not abuse the great power entrusted unto me."

But very little aesthetic appreciation will be required to realise that in these rituals are passages of divine beauty and high eloquence. And the least learned will find ideas of especial appeal to him, as the scholar and the profound mystic will perceive great depth and erudition in what may appear on the surface as simple statement. Properly performed, these rituals are stately ceremonies of great inspiration and enlightenment.

With each of the grades just described, a certain amount of personal work was provided, principally of a theoretical kind. The basic ideas of the Qabalah were imparted by means of so-called knowledge lectures, together with certain important symbols, and significant names in Hebrew were required to be memorized. The lamens—insignia worn over the heart—of the various Officers were referred in divers ways to the Tree of Life, thus explaining after a fashion the function of that particular offiice in the Temple of Initiation. Each path traversed, and every grade entered, had a so-called Admission Badge. This usually consisted of one of the many forms of the Cross, and of symbols of the type of the Swastika, truncated Pyramid, and so forth. To these astrological, and elemental attributions were referred. Most of these symbols possess great value, and since they repeatedly recur under different guises through the stages of personal magical work undertaken after the Adeptus Minor grade, they should receive the benefit of prolonged brooding and meditation.

Three of the most important items of personal study to be accomplished while in the First or Outer Order, apart from the memorisation of the rudiments of the Qabalah were: (a) The practice of the Pentagram Ritual with the Qabalistic Cross, (b) Tatwa Vision, and (c) Divination by Geomancy and the simple Tarot method described by Waite in his *Key to the Tarot*.

Originally, the Pentagram Ritual was taught to the Neophyte immediately after his initiation in order that he might "form some idea of how to attract and come into communication with spiritual and invisible things." Just as the Neophyte Ceremony of admission contains the essential symbolism of the Great Work, shadowing forth symbolically the commencement of certain formulae of the Magic of Light, so potential within the Pentagram

Ritual and the Qabalistic Cross are the epitomes of the whole of that work. In all magical procedure is it fundamental, for it is a gesture of upraising the human consciousness to its own root of perfection and enlightenment by which the sphere of sensation and every act performed under its surveillance are sanctified. Thus it should precede every phase of magical work, elementary as well as advanced. The written rubric has previously appeared in my *Tree of Life*, and I may now add a word or two concerning the further directions which are orally imparted to the Candidate after his admission.

The prime factor towards success in that exercise is to imagine that the astral form is capable of expansion, that it grows tall and high, until at length it has the semblance of a vast angelic figure, whose head towers amongst the distant stars of heaven. When this imaginative expansion of consciousness produces the sense that the height is enormous, with the Earth as a tiny globe revolving beneath the feet, then above the head should be perceived or formulated a descending ray of brilliant Light. As the candidate marks the head and then the breast, so should this brilliance descend, even down to his feet, a descending shaft of a gigantic cross of Light. The act of marking the shoulders right and left whilst vibrating the Sephirotic names, traces the horizontal shaft of the cross, equilibrating the Light within the sphere of sensation. Since it has been argued above that the Great Work consists in the search for the Light, this ritual truly and completely performed leads to the accomplishment of that Work and the personal discovery of the Light. The Pentagrams trace a cleansing and protecting circle of force invoked by the four Names of four letters each about the limits of the personal sphere, and the Archangels are called, by vibration, to act as great stabilising influences.

The study of the different types of divination may seem difficult to understand in an Order which purported to teach methods of spiritual development. Many will no doubt be rather perplexed by this. Divination usually is said to refer exclusively to the low occult arts, to fortune-telling, and the prognostication of the future. Actually, however, so far as the Order is concerned, the principal object for these practical methods is that they stimulate, as few exercises can, the faculties of clairvoyance, imagination, and intuition. Though certain readings or interpretations to the geomantic and Tarot symbols may be found in the appropriate text books, these rule of thumb methods do not conduce to the production of an accurate delineation of the spiritual causes behind material events. These interpretations are usual to the beginner in the art, for he requires a foundation of the principal definitions employed upon which his own meditations can build. These textual delineations serve in actual practice only as a base for the working of the inner faculties, provides for them a thrust-block as it were from which they may "kick-off." In short, the effort to divine by these methods calls into operation the intuitive and imaginative faculties to a very large extent. Everyone without exception has this faculty of divining in some degree, varying only in his ability to make it manifest. In most people it is wholly dormant.

Again, while divination as an artificial process may be wholly unnecessary and a hindrance to the refined perceptions of a fully developed Adept, who requires no such convention to ascertain whence a thing comes and whither it is going, yet these aids and stimuli have their proper place for the Neophyte. For those in training they are not only legitimate but useful and necessary. It may be interesting for the reader to attempt to acquire intuitive knowledge on any matter without the divinatory aids first, and it will be seen how extremely difficult it is to get started, to pick upon any one fact or incident which shall act as a prompt or a starter of the interior mechanism. Having failed in this way, let him see how much further he really may go by the judicious and sensible use of one of the Order methods. There is no doubt that the opening of the mind to an intuitive perception is considerably aided by these methods. And this is particularly true with regard to the rather lengthy Tarot method which was given to the initiate while engaged in the fulfiment of his Adeptus Minor curriculum. Like all magical techniques, divination is open to abuse. The fact, however, that abuse is possible does not as again and again must be reiterated fully condemn the abused technique. The application of commonsense to the magical art is as necessary as it is to all else.

There is a movement on foot in one of the Temples to eliminate the study and practice of Geomancy from the scheme of training of the Outer Order. The prevailing tendency is so to simplify the road to Adeptship as to reduce the practical requisites to an absolute minimum by eliminating every phase of the work which does not come "naturally", and whose study might involve hard work. Most of the newly admitted candidates to this Temple within the past five years or more are utterly without any practical acquaintance with this technipue.

Originally, Astrology was taught as part of the regular routine. All instruction on this subject seems now to have been thoroughly extirpated from the Order papers. Perhaps in this particular instance the omission is just as well. For recent years have seen a great deal of meticulous attention paid to this study by sincere and honest researchers, and there have been published many first-rate books explaining its intricacies. All that the Order demands of the Adeptus Minor is that he should understand the underlying principles of this science, and be able to draw up a map showing the position of Planets and Signs preparatory to certain operations requiring the invocation of zodiacal forces.

Tatwa vision requires but little mention in this place,

for in this book's sequel *The Golden Dawn*, now in the press, will be found full instructions in this technical method of acquiring clairvoyance. They are compiled from a number of documents and verbal instructions obtaining within the Order. Since these oral "tit-bits" and papers were very scattered, it has been found necessary to reorganise the whole matter. In that restatement, however, I have exercised no originality nor uttered personal viewpoints on any phase of the technique, confining my labour solely to re-writing the material in my possession. It may be interesting for the psychological critic to reflect upon the fact that it was this technique to which most members of the Order devoted the greatest attention—the only technique in which, more than any other single branch of the work, there is the greatest opportunity for deception and self-deception. While in many ways the Order technique may appear different from the vision method described in my *Tree of Life*, both are essentially the same. For they teach the necessity of an imaginative formation of an intellectual or astral form, the Body of Light, for the purpose of exploring the different regions of the Tree of Life or the several strata of one's own psychic make-up. The simplest aspects of this investigation are taught just after the grade of Philosophus, though naturally the full possibilities of this method and the complete details on the technical side do not reveal themselves until the teaching of the Second Order has been received.

In addition to these technical methods there were meditations on the symbols and ideas of the whole system, and it was quite frequently suggested that the student go through the ceremonies, after having taken the grades, and build them up in his imagination so that he relives them as vividly as when he was in the Temple. The practical exercise that accompanied the Portal grade was one in which the aspirant built up, again in the imagination, a symbolic form of the Tree of Life, paying particular attention to the formation of the Middle Pillar, in the sphere of sensation or aura. This latter was conceived to be an ovoid shape of subtle matter, and the formulation of the various Sephiroth therein while vibrating the appropriate divine names went far towards opening, in a safe and balanced way, the psycho-spiritual centres of which the Sephiroth were symbols. Not without a certain sense of hesitancy do I say that this practice with its development is one of the most important in the entire Order curriculum. This technique I have described and considerably amplified in my book "The Middle Pillar."

Here, then, is a brief outline, a bird's eye view of the routine of the grades and practice as established in the First or Outer Order of the Golden Dawn. The graduated training of the entire Order was intended as a preparation for the practical work to be performed in the Inner or Second Order of the Roseae Rubeae et Aureae Crucis. The assignation of personal magical work seems deliberately to have been postponed until after the Vault reception. It was considered that the Ceremony formulated a link between the Aspirant and his Augoeides, that connection serving therefore as a guide and a powerful protection which is clearly required in the works of Ceremonial Magic. Since at the commencement of each serious operation the initiate must needs exalt himself towards his higher and divine Genius, that through him may flow the divine power which alone is capable of producing a pure magical work, the initial forging of that link is a matter of supreme importance.

The apparent complexity of the above delineated scheme may be thought by some individuals to be entirely too complicated and not sufficiently simple in nature. While one can deeply sympathise with the ideals of the extreme simplicity cult in Mysticism, nevertheless it is evident that the complex and arduous nature of the routine is no fault of Magic. Man himself is responsible for this awkward situation. By reason of countless centuries of evolution and material development — sometimes in quite false directions—man has spiritually repressed himself and thus gradually forgotten his true divine nature. Meanwhile, as a sort of compensation for this loss, he has developed a complexity of physical and psychic constitution for dealing adequately with the physical world. Hence, methods of spiritual development refusing to admit the reality of that many-principled organisation may not be recognised as valid, for the sole reason that man is not a simple being. Having strayed from his roots, and lost his spiritual birthright in a jungle of delusion, it is not always easy to re-discover those roots or to find the way out from the Gates of the Land of Night. Magic recognises the many-faceted nature of Man. If that intricate structure be an evil, as some seem to think, it is a necessary evil. It is one to be faced and used, and therefore Magic connives by its technique to develop and improve each of those several principles to its highest degree of perfection. Not enough is it to be illuminated. The problem is not as simple as that. It is in vain that the wine of the Gods is poured into broken bottles. Each part of the soul, each elemental aspect of the entire man must be strengthened and transmuted, and brought into equilibrium and harmony with the others. Integration must be the rule of the initiate, not pathology. In such a vehicle made consecrate and truly holy by this equilibriation, the higher Genius may find a worthy and fit dwelling. This, and this alone, may ever constitute the true nature of the Adept.

CHAPTER FOUR

DARKNESS

Having now briefly reviewed the whole cycle of the Order system with its ceremonial grades as it is in theory, let me now devote some little space to analysing the practice of the Order as it exists in reality. It should be most impressive, the reader may think, to celebrate these Rituals and witness their performance in the proper atmosphere and circumstance of the Temple. Indeed they are. Few things could be more satisfying to the inner sense. There have been occasions, however, when those rituals have been heard recited with about as much feeling and enthusiasm or sense of their intrinsic value as one would impart to the checking of a butcher's account. It is appalling how little emphasis was given to these important matters of delivery, for in an impressive though not necessarily theatrical delivery lies one of the easiest ways of driving the rituals' instruction into the mind and sphere of the candidate. Of course, it must be understood that my present criticisms are not directed towards ordinary instances of self-consciousness on the part of a newly instituted officer.

Considered from one angle, that is the danger of all ceremonial. It is too apt to degenerate into ritual—using that word in its worst sense, the performance of practices or customs of any kind without thought or intention, stultifying formalisms. Attacks on ceremonial systems are only too often justified. The mere formal ritualistic performances of these or any other ceremony, from which every vestige of meaning has departed, is not of assistance to any being but a source of real danger and spiritual bondage. Rituals also, perfunctorily performed, and without enthusiasm, are void of virtue, need never have been celebrated, and fail utterly to initiate.

In the Zelator grade, for example, there occurs this rather splendid passage: "And Tetragrammaton placed Kerubim at the East of the Garden of Eden and a Flaming Sword which turned every way to keep the path of the Tree of Life, for He has created Nature that man being cast out of Eden may not fall into the Void. He has bound man with the stars as with a chain. He allures him with scattered fragments of the Divine Body in bird and beast and flower. And He laments over him in the Wind and in the Sea and in the birds. When the times are ended, He will call the Kerubim from the East of the Garden, and all shall be consumed and become infinite and holy." But from the manner in which this and similar passages were read, one would never have realised that a marvellous promise of beauty and high eloquence and lofty significance had been presented to one's consciousness.

The writer also remembers clearly being at one grade ceremony, that of Philosophus in point of fact, where several ecstatic and stirring passages occur, particularly in the traversal of the Path of Mars. These passages from one of the Psalms were deliberately included to work up a vibrant atmosphere, provided to create a sense of energy and excitement, appropriate to the presence of a fiery martial force. When the ceremony was over and the opportunity presented itself to glance through the ritual, it amazed me to note how slurred and unimaginative had been the renderings of most of the lines: "The River Kishon swept them away—that Ancient River, the River Kishon. O my soul, thou hast trodden down strength." "He bowed the heavens also, and came down, and the darkness was under his feet. At the brightness that was before him, the thick clouds passed—hailstones and flashings of fire. The Lord thundered through the heavens and the Highest gave forth his voice—hailstones and flashings of fire. He sent out his arrows and scattered them. He hurled forth his lightnings and destroyed them." It does not concern me for the time being to argue whether or not a profound meaning inheres within these biblical verses. What is important is that they impart atmosphere. Properly recited in the tense atmosphere of the Temple, when the candidate is enormously keyed up and where anything apparently could or might happen, and where previously the Fire elementals have been invoked, there is a quality within these words which actually and not merely figuratively thrills. And unless this dynamic thrill is imparted by the vibration and vigorous enthusiasm of this invocation, for such it is, then the ceremony must be set aside as having failed in effect. It *must* communicate a thrill, for apart from all else the rite is conducting the candidate through the Path of Mars, where there should be fire and energy and excitement literally vibrating within the air. If the candidate does respond or is *made* to respond to the invocation so that he is strangely stirred to that music and an excitement springs up from the depths of his soul, then the force which previously had been invoked may properly impinge upon his nature and awaken its corresponding aspect within his being.

Certain phases and functions of ritual have much in common with the *koan* technique of Zen Buddhism. "The *koan* is a word or phrase or saying which has certain qualities, the most important being that it defies intellectual analysis and thereby enables the user to burst the fetters of conceptual thought." It is a psychic riddle before which the mind darkens, and in the cessation of conscious thought which should thereupon ensue, the student should be hurled by the impetus of the apparently ridiculous *koan* into the exaltation of the mystical experience. It is my belief that the exalting phrases and dramatic passages

96

which occur in some of the magical rituals are of this nature, and their quality is such that provided they are intoned with even a minimum of vigour and enthusiasm the candidate should be strongly affected.

There was a much more serious blunder of a similar kind in a ceremony of the Second Order. More prominently than many other memories, there stands out in my mind my personal reception to the grade of Adeptus Minor. I have already explained that this ritual is the jewel in the crown of the Order ceremonial system, that this Ritual is without a doubt the finest and most effectual one of that particular type possessed by the Order, its purpose being the forging of a true link between the aspirant and his higher Genius. In the first point of the ceremony shortly after the admission, the candidate is affixed to a large upstanding Cross, the Cross of Obligation. Thereon, under the most solemn circumstances, he is obliged to assume a sacred vow. The officiating Adept reads several phrases first, and the candidate in turn repeats them. It is not difficult to realise that this is a critical and important phase of the Ceremony. During this Obligation, because of the symbolism attached to it, and because of the active aspiration which is induced at this juncture, illumination may quite easily occur. Provided, of course, that the officers do their part. Actually, Frater D.D.C.F. recorded in a paper dealing with the symbolism of this grade that the object of the ceremony conceived as a whole "is especially intended to effect the change of the consciousness into the Neschamah, and there are three places where this can take place. The first is when the aspirant is on the Cross, because he is so exactly fulfilling the symbol of the abnegation of the lower self and the Union with the Higher Self."

Moreover, the preface to the assumption of the obligation is under these circumstances a tremendously impressive occurrence, and few could fail to be even faintly moved by it. It consists of an invocation of an Angelic power: "In the divine name IAO, I invoke Thee, the great avenging Angel HUA, that thou mayest invisibly place Thy hand upon the head of this Aspirant in attestation of his obligation." Yet, in practice, this obligation—one of the three major events of the ceremony—was hurried through with as much speed as could legitimately be given, and babbled as quickly as the words themselves could be enunciated. As though it were a mere formality, an insignificant gesture without meaning of any kind, was this uttered. The Chiefs of the Temple were present, and I know none called this particular Frater to task that he might fulfil his high office in more seemly and becoming manner.

It also came to my hearing from one of the Chiefs that these identical tactics were pursued at the equally impressive consecration of the Vault on Corpus Christi day of last year. As a result the ceremony which was conducted on behalf of the whole fraternity was dead. The Temple never became enlivened with the flashing force that should have manifested itself. No power was generated in any way. The ceremony became a meaningless perfunctory piece of formalism, the Chief Adept simply mumbling his speeches as though anxious to be through with it, and nothing more. So far as concerned any benefit accruing to the Order by this ceremony, it was nothing but a waste of time and energy. This officer was an Adeptus Exemptus!

When originally the English Temples were instituted by the trio of Woodman, Westcott and Mathers, the grade system they inaugurated was completed by the taking of the Adeptus Minor ceremony. There were no grades beyond that. With the admission to the Second Order, the aspirant received a curriculum of the complete magical training which it was his duty to perform alone and apply to his own spiritual make-up. In reality, the work given is a complete and admirable system. It is herein that the highest conceptions of Theurgy are exhibited. There is little doubt in my mind that assiduously applied and followed in all its branches that training, applied with initiative, may lead the sincere aspirant a very long way on the Path towards Adeptship. In the curriculum of work prescribed for the Zelator Adeptus Minor, there is sufficient to keep all but the spiritual genius—of whom, alas, there are but few amongst us—occupied and very busy for the remainder of their lives. Beyond the formulae contained in the documents listed on a later page there is no need to seek help. The system is complete, provided of course it is studied and applied. In a note in my possession from the Imperator of one of the Temples, it is remarked that "we have practically no formulae about Tiphareth. I suppose the idea is that by then you should be capable of making your own." Obviously, if Adeptship means anything at all.

Vanity, however, is the incurable curse of mankind, and of occult students especially. It has always been so insidious that a simple system of the type originally instituted must be hedged about with every kind of proviso. By the time most candidates have passed through the preliminary six grades of the First Order, they have become confirmed in the expectancy of further grades. Should there be none, quite often they become highly disappointed. It seems useless pointing out that spiritual attainment has value and significance, and that grades have none. Nor would any good be accomplished by emphasising the implication of the grades and the magical spheres they signify. Most students do not appear to realise exactly what is meant by the term Adept, greater or lesser, nor why a severe discipline and training embracing every branch of man's nature should be so absolutely necessary, a discipline which is indicated by the whole of the tradition. For most it is simply an honorific title, a grade conferred by a ceremony. That is why so few have any hesitancy in accepting further grades and claiming high degrees of Adeptship.

One of the principal errors, it seems to me, lies in the present allocation of grades to the Sephiroth. Or rather, the failure is in the lack of emphasis on, or the refusal fully to appreciate, the warning contained in the Portal grade, where it is distinctly pointed out that the four elemental grades "quit not Malkuth." Hence, theoretically as well as actually, the Philosophus, to take an example, has not elevated his consciousness to the spiritual height of Netzach simply through a series of symbolic movements in a Temple. He has only become aware of the particular correspondence of Netzach in so far as it reflects or imparts a fiery quality to his Malkuth. Justification seems to exist for this assumption by the very way in which the Minutum Mundum portrays Malkuth. It depicts Malkuth in four sections, each attributed to the operation of one of the elements, and consequently to one of the grades. Since the ceremonies are clearly but *reflections* of possible experiences, symbolic rpresentations of a spiritual journey towards the Light, and since the outer grades are unmistakeably referred to Malkuth, technically the Adeptus Minor grade, with that of the Portal, is a *reflection* in Yesod of the attainment of Tiphareth. It therefore cannot confer any degree of Adeptship. In Yesod is the operation of the Moon which *reflects* the rays of the Sun. It is also the sphere of the Astral Light, the so-called Hall of Learning, the plane of phantasy, dream and deception. It is one of the subtlest forms of deception which has overtaken the Order in that its members almost without a single exception have mistaken the reflection for the reality. That they really have become Adepts through the ceremony is soberly believed by the members themselves. In point of fact, the grade should just make one aware of that lengthy road which the Adept must

100

follow, and the arduous task to be performed if some reality is to be given to the treading of that Path. Though I am in accord with the widely held view that by means of the ceremony a condition is induced in the candidate, which, if he is otherwise prepared, may enable him to enter the sphere of a real experience, yet the emphasis must be laid on the expression "if he is otherwise prepared." And I am fully convinced that while the initiation ceremonies are of inestimable assistance, the implicit attainment of the grade is only manifested and made explicit by means of the prolonged training and spiritual labour which should follow.

Regardless of this, it was very early in the history of the Order that discontent made itself noticed because there were no higher grades than that of Adeptus Minor. In 1892, therefore, says Dr. Westcott in his pamphlet on Rosicrucian history, Frater D.D.C.F. "supplied the Ritual of an Adept grade from materials obtained from a Frater L.E.T., a continental Adept." This grade, I assume, was that of Adeptus Major. It was installed as a regular part of the routine, an interval of five years being required to elapse between the grade of Adeptus Minor and the passage to the new grade. Beyond the facts just mentioned I know absolutely nothing of this grade of Adeptus Major. And care less. For the facts are, as anyone will understand who has the least sympathy for and insight into the requisites of Magic and Mysticism, that the work concentrated about the Adeptus Minor attainment can hardly be performed in its entirety within five years save by those who have unlimited time at their disposal, as well as an extraordinary flair for the subject. Whether the present body of Adepti of the Order have this latter qualification is a thing which is to be strongly doubted, though many of them were favoured by the former. From the Order history one questions whether any of the Adepti ever possessed that requisite or at any

101

time gave the term Adeptship any real significance.

The same insidious vanity, moreover, and the same discontent which had demanded the addition of the Adeptus Major grade made it imperative that further grades should be affixed to the system. It was not, of course, that the members had become such greatly exalted Adepts and had arrived at such a spiritual stature that there was nothing further in the then extant Order work which could assist them. It was simply vanity—for many of them had received the Adeptus Major grade without having performed all the necessary work of the preceding Adept grade. Further grades then being demanded it was only natural that they should be forthcoming. Necessity is said to be the mother of invention, and supply likewise can be made to equal the demand. It was many years after the rebellion when all was chaos with the Order split into several warring factions, each contriving to prove itself superior to the other, that this imperious desire for more grades arose. Consequently, Frater F. R. with a colleague, I believe, travelled to the Continent in search of grades. There, so we are informed, he contacted and entered into fraternal communion with a certain secret body. Because it was a secret body and because it purported to be Rosicrucian, it was assumed *ex hypothesi* to be that indentical source from which Woodman and Westcott originally obtained authority for the commencement of the English Temples. Temporarily forgotten was the fact that at one time Germany was overrun with so-called Rosicrucian bodies. As Franz Hartmann wrote many years ago in his work *In the Pronaos of the Temple*: "As the people became infatuated with the idea of becoming Rosicrucians and no real society of Adepts could be found, they organised Rosicrucian societies without any real Adepts, and thus a great many so-called Rosicrucian societies came into existence." That the rituals of this particular body discovered by Frater F.R. bore various resemblances to those of the Order, as naturally they would, seems to have caused him to overlook an important fact which might have occurred to most students. That fact is that a more or less complete exposition of the Vault of Christian Rosenkreutz, for example, is contained in the *Fama Fraternatitas,* and many groups no doubt made use of that fundamental material. It would not be a difficult matter compiling Rituals of initiation once one has access to a certain literature and once one has assimilated something of the correspondences of the Qabalistic system. However, from this organisation Frater F.R. obtained certain material which he systematised and formed into rituals upon his return to England just before the War.

Quite apart from these considerations as to the genuineness of the Rituals, whether he or any of his colleagues who seceded from Mathers were competent or fit guides in the matter of ritualism, is in my opinion open to question. Some little while ago, there was passed on to me a Consecration Ritual which originated, so I understand, with Frater F.R. It made use of the Rite of the Kerubic Stations of the Theoricus Grade where, to invoke the powers of the Astral—the primordial archetypes of the Collective Unconscious—occurs this passage: "Give me your hands O ye Lords of Truth, for I am made as ye are," etc. Someone without the least appreciation of the value of words, without discretion even, had altered this in the Consecration Ritual to "Extend to me your hands" etc.

No doubt it was this same individual, be it F.R. or another, who was responsible for several alterations in the Neophyte grade. Originally, as practised before the schism, one phrase went: "And the voice of my higher Self said unto me" etc. This was altered into: "The voice of my undying and secret soul!" Again, in that same ritual, the injunction of the Hiereus to the Candidate at one time read, "Fear is failure, and the forerunner of failure.

103

Be thou therefore without fear. For in the heart of the coward virtue abideth not." The later version used by the Stella Matutina and irresponsibly changed is: "Fear is failure, be thou therefore without fear. For he who trembles at the flame, and at the flood, and at the shadows of the air, hath no part in God." How infinitely superior and psychologically more adequate is the earlier version? I think mention ought to be made of the change of this phrase: "I declare that the Sun has risen and the shadows flee away." The words "Day star" were substituted for the "Sun." They were not content with simplicity.

To return, however. Meaningless strings of laudatory titles conferring the higher Adept degrees were added to the original simple system of grades which had culminated in the Vault with the reception into the Roseae Rubeae et Aureae Crucis. In my examination book in which were noted the signatures of the Chiefs to several examinations passed may be seen appended to the motto of one signatory the incredible figures of $9 = 2$, the grade of Magus referred to Chokmah! Another of the signatories signed herself as $7 = 4$—that is the grade of Adeptus Exemptus, referred to Chesed. Whilst a third appears as Theoricus Adeptus Minor $7 = 4$. It is to such ridiculous heights of vanity and fantasy that the members of the Order were sometimes accustomed to look for advice and guidance.

These were great Adepts. When one contemplates the fact—and since the curriculum of work is reproduced herein, this fact can now be realised by the reader—that in the Adeptus Minor grade is enough work to occupy one for many years, if one is honest, it escapes me wholly how any student of the divine wisdom can have the temerity and impertinence to lay claim to these grotesqueries. One of the Chiefs of the Temple, in a thoroughly objectionable and complacent mood, once smugly confided in the writer that "most of our members, you know, are quite satisfied not to go much beyond the grade of Adeptus Minor." This, of course, was an implication intended to be subtle, that she was wrapped in veils of the highest sanctity and that the real attainment of Adeptship was an adolescent growth above which she had long since been exalted. Yet, ironically enough, frequent conversations and repeated enquiries for information concerning fundamental issues of the mere Adeptus Minor work, elementary stuff one would have thought, elicited not the least satisfaction.

The root of the trouble, quite apart from the grade misconceptions as well as the curse of vanity, was of course that the work was only cursorily performed. No one really cared a fig for Magic and spiritual development. No one really strived for mastery of any technique. Grades, and grades alone, were the goal. One of the things which stands uppermost amongst my memories in this connection is the abuse of the examination system. The latter obviously is a mechanism for ensuring the possession of certain items of knowledge. The candidate was required to pass frequent examinations in theoretical knowledge. He was tested in memorised material, as well as in his ability to skry in the spirit vision, to divine by various methods, and also in his magical power to consecrate the various implements required for his practical occult work. It would be thoroughly absurd to suppose, first, that a single performance of these latter consecration ceremonies taught all that there is to be known about consecrations. The reader can be assured that it is a highly complex matter, and it requires an enormous amount of practice before one even begins to realise what are the fundamental factors involved. Or, secondly, that the psychological or spiritual noumena of these weapons had actually been built up or awakened within the soul through but a single ceremonial effort. Or, thirdly, that because one has obtained a few Tatwa visions, and has made and ceremonially consecrated a Lotus Wand, a Rose-Cross lamen, a sword and four Elemental weapons, that the work of Adeptship is completed. Yet pretty much this attitude was common. This was the sole requirement to complete the sub-grade of Zelator Adeptus Minor. Very few that the writer has encountered ever thought of repeating the consecration ceremonies. Many have been elevated to higher grades on hardly greater attainment than that.

Any reasonably intelligent person can be trained and shown how to do these simple consecration ceremonies. Those with a particularly good mechanical memory would experience no trouble with the divinatory methods. Clairvoyance—surely that alone is far from proof of Adeptship? The Order of the Golden Dawn has had within its portals innumerable psychics and clairvoyants—many of them I must hasten to add of a very fine calibre. While clairvoyance *may* be and actually is of inestimable service to the Great Work, its possession does not in itself point to attainment or spirituality. In fact, the purely spiritual application of clairvoyance to Rising on the Planes, skrying in the highest Paths of the Tree of Life, acquiring the Visions and initiations of the innermost of the Thirty Aethyrs—these were seldom done. Just enough work was performed for examination purposes. Clairvoyance is spiritually useful in intelligent and aspiring possession. But its assignation exclusively to psychic ends is useless. These ends have brought degradation to the Order. Most of its clairvoyant members are, with only one or two possible exceptions, mere Astral tramps—psychic nymphomaniacs. Any individual who has an ordinary visualising faculty can be taught by the Order methods to induce lucidity of a positive kind within a short while. Most women have this faculty of thinking in pictures, of forming mental images, to a marked degree—thus the majority of the Order clairvoyants were women. And because clairvoyance came to be so highly prized, it was not to be wondered at that the offices of the Chiefs and the important posts in many Temples came to be occupied by women. Without wishing to subscribe in any shape or form to misogyny, such a policy is fatal to any occult organisation, as has been proved over and over again.

Incidentally, it may be as well to attempt to thrash out a distinction between imagination and visualisation which seem always hopelessly confused. There was ever in the Order a good deal of glibness about 'creative imagination'. As may be imagined, this was seldom if ever displayed. The lack of eloquence in ceremonial, the petrification of the true spirit of the Order, the elimination of vital knowledge from official routine, the inability to realise essential points of magical technique, these are unperjurable witnesses to the fact that never once was imagination permitted to rear its head. On the other hand, there was an ample representation of the visual faculty, and of course of clairvoyance. But imagination was a creative faculty of mind which is akin to genius. From what I can gather it may or may not be accompanied by the ability to form clear-cut mental pictures or images. Creative imagination could well have been employed to expand and develop the skeletal elements of the Order system. There are several aspects of the technique which are urgently in need of imaginative research to place them on a sound and acceptable footing. On the contrary, there was only an ignorant tearing down, a lamentable withdrawing of documents, and a persistent refusal to perform immensely important rituals within the sphere of personal training. Fear probably was responsible. And this despite the first injunction that the Neophyte in the Order hears: "Fear is failure and the forerunner of failure. Be thou therefore without fear. For in the heart of the coward virtue abideth not." That most of the Adepti were moral cowards has long been recognised, for they were completely and utterly afraid of Magic in all its branches. They contented themselves with the mild celebration of the initiation ceremonies, an occasional debauch in the realm of divination, and were satisfied with simple visions of the Tatwa type—an anthropoid simulation of enlightenment. Certain there was no virtue in the Order. Whether the lust for advanced grades may be construed as an indication of imagination, or simply the very ordinary manifestation of vanity, fantasy, and cupidity, must not be left to me to decide.

It was MacGregor Mathers who, shortly after the development of the schism, uttered these memorable words —true not only of the revolting members of his day but having even greater application to the, whom Crowley aptly called, Inepti of the present moment. "I admit that I have committed one great though unavoidable fault, which is this. In giving these persons so great a knowledge I have not also been able to give them brains and intelligence to comprehend it, for this miracle the Gods have not granted me the power to perform. You had better address your approaches to the Gods, rather than to me, unless some spark of returning wisdom can make you recognise in such critics' the swine who trample the divine teachings under foot." Fully do I recognise and admit that Mathers was responsible for a number of unpardonable deeds. His scholarship at times is alleged to have been faulty. He may have been incompetent and irresponsible as a leader, as still others claim. Nevertheless, it is my firm conviction, and I feel impelled to register it strongly, that there was more magic capacity and spiritual insight within the least part of his frame than has the entire sterile Adept body of the Stella Matutina. Concealed within the Order documents is a vast wisdom, true secrets, indicible, and incapable of being communicated. A vast wisdom never perceived by those whose lust is for higher grades. A wisdom not seen by those whose sole concern is with the careful elimination of important rituals, and who occupy themselves with the knowledge of such petty trifles as the number and width and type of the several curves in the body of the Serpent of Wisdom.

One of the fundamental techniques to which little or no attention was bestowed in the Order was that of the Angelic or Enochian Tablets. Beyond demonstrating the dubious ingenuity of a certain Adeptus Exemptus in the matter of re-writing in the form of a concise resumé the rather scattered incrustions produced by Mathers and Westcott, but which had previously been cleverly systematised by another student, there was hereon very little practical work performed. Yet it is evident that a very great deal of the other Order routine has its basis and root herein. Regardless of its obscure origins—and they are highly obscure—the formulae of the truncated pyramid, Egyptian god-form, and the elemental sphinx involved in the analysis and skrying of the Watchtower squares are among the most profound magical techniques ever devised. The Enochian system demonstrates, as nothing else does, the amazing ingenuity and fertility of the synthetic genius peculiar to the Golden Dawn. Accompanying these Angelic Tablets are a series of Enochian invocations or Calls as they are sometimes called. The offiicial instruction remarks of them that "though these Calls are thus to be employed to aid thee in the skrying of the Tablets in the Spirit-Vision, and in magical working therewith, yet shalt thou know that they may be allotted unto a much higher plane than the operation of the Tablets in the Asiatic world. And therefore are they thus employed in bringing the higher Light and the all-potent forces into action herein." Instead of wasting no inconsiderable length of time with the wild-goose chase after grades or astral masters, one might have supposed that attention paid to some such technical method of development would have yielded important spiritual results. But apart from Crowley I have never made the acquaintance of a single initiate of the Adeptus Minor or any other grade who had ever made the effort to investigate the possibilities of bringing the higher Light into operation by means of this system.

Even the ordinary elementary techniques of the dogmatic or theoretical Qabalah were glossed over in an inconceivable way so that neglect of the more magical aspects of the system should not surprise one very much. The knowledge lectures deliberately give the numbers and symbols referred to the Hebrew Letters. It was believed by one of the Adepti that perhaps the Gematria of the Names and Ages of the Three early Chiefs of the Order might contain some significance as indicating a formula of Magic. But this Adept, despite almost twenty years of membership was utterly without any kind of knowledge as to how to proceed and what methods to employ in the Qabalistic development of this idea. There was just ingenuity enough to convert the Hebrew letters into the Tarot equivalents and that was all.

Another fact imperfectly recognised by the Adepti is that the consecration of implements which is the principal work prescribed for the first stage of the Adeptus Minor grade, concerns when all is said and done the technique of talismans. A talisman is a symbol or symbolic object —a jewel, metal, a circular piece of vellum or parchment —charged or impregnated with the particular force which is referred to it. One definition describes a talisman as a "dead thing, impure, valueless and powerless" which by means of Magic, that is an act of will, usually ceremonially operated, is transformed into "a live thing, active, invaluable and thaumaturgic." The symbol or object itself has not the least value. That is why every form of commerce in amulets and charms is so utterly despicable. The talisman is powerless until it has been consecrated and been made the vehicle of the appropriate type of forces. In fact, the attainment of the spiritual knowledge of the higher and divine Genius may also be considered to come

110

under the general significance of the formulae of Talismanic Magic. For the lower self may be considered as the symbol, impure and powerless, and the higher Genius as the thaumaturgic transforming power, while the conjunction of these two selves caused by the descent of the latter, forms a species of charged talisman. It is a particular instance of a general formula. Other instances are the techniques of the Eucharist and Healing as well as the art of conferring Initiation.

Now though the consecration of weapons was an important because fundamental task, there was absolutely no information forthcoming about this obscure matter other than a few very trite observations in one of the unofficial documents. Long previously the Chiefs of the Temple had charged their own instruments, as well as superintendended for many years the magical efforts of their successors, yet still nothing was known definitely about the art of consecration. A question fired point-blank to a Chief as to whether talismans had been known to produce any verified result simply evoked "I don't know." And while this answer may be appreciated by some for its absolute honesty and valued by others as evidence of the worthlessness of the whole system, infinitely more than all else it indicates an inability or a blind refusal to analyse the work constantly being done. An inability to develop logically the technique whose fundamentals had been placed in their hands. And this, let me add, despite constant references *ad nauseam* to so-called scientific methods and the marvellous progress of modern psychology.

It is difficult to account for this curious lack of information concerning fundamental techniques. Perhaps we may attribute as partly responsible the prolonged and adamant refusal to preserve any record of previous investigations in the divine science, or to be guided by those accumulations of record in subsequent experiment and practical

111

developmental work. To test and to verify the generalisations derived from the experience of one's forebearers constitutes an important step towards the organisation of a well-defined body of knowledge. It is in this progressive attitude where lies the virtue of the so-called scientific method. Each generation of scientists is thus able to begin where its predecessors left off, without having to retrace its footsteps unnecessarily. If however no organised body of knowledge is kept, no organised science that is based upon traditional theory and teaching, then manifestly there can be no constructive policy for the teaching itself. This perhaps may explain why the Order system after nearly fifty years of constant practice has never become an established and recognised cultural factor. This crippling point of view was once formally and officially stated in these words: "It is against the traditions of the Order to keep much of the personal records lest they become dogma that students accept rather than make the effort to do their own experimenting."

While it is seriously to be doubted that this is the Order tradition—being only a personal viewpoint to cover up very interesting unconscious motives—certainly the explanation seems a plausible one. Something could possibly be said in its favour. It is quite conceivable that an examination of former experiences may act somewhat in the manner of suggestion. This may result in the subsequent experiences and experiments of the injudicious student being coloured and tempered by what he has read. Were blue pigs mentioned in an official document, some credulous member would certainly produce a vision concerning those same blue pigs.

Thus this withholding of former experiences is justifiable in a subject which is almost exclusively psychological and interior.

Actually, however, if a little reflection is given to it, the whole argument is specious and empty. It consists solely of meretricious phrases. Can one imagine the nature of a study of Philosophy which did not enunciate dialectical principles which had been introduced into historical metaphysic by Plato and Leibnitz, Kant and Hegel? Have Descartes, Hume and Schopenhauer, for example, reasoned and written wholly in vain that their names and philosophies should deliberately be withheld from us? How barren and sterile would that study be! What form, also, would academic Psychology assume were present-day students not informed as to the epoch-making and pioneer work of such researchers as Freud and Jung? And to what banal insignificance would psychology sink were we not aware of the classical cases which were responsible for those monumental discoveries in the world of the psyche? Indeed, one questions whether there could really be a science of any kind without such a historical body of experimental record being always available and to which further evidence is continually being appended. In fact, the first phase of study in such a sphere must consist primarily of an examination of the work of our predecessors so as to realise the historical continuity of scientific or philosophical endeavour, and to perceive our rightful place at the summit of a vast pyramid of experimental work. Upon this foundation we may proceed with original work. Could it be argued that because our scientists and psychologists have had access to the records of previous investigators that the pioneer spirit of investigation has been killed? Such a point of view is puerile. It is too absurd to warrant further argument.

It is clearly for this fundamental reason that the Order has utterly failed to raise its traditional heritage to the status of an accredited science. It is hardly that Magic is not amenable to scientific treatment, for nothing could be further from the truth. This failure must be laid at the hands of a few individuals in whose hands the governance of the modern Temples has fallen. And I can only suggest that it was their ineptitude and their spiritual emptiness which is responsible for this false and short-sighted attitude. Though I have every reason to believe that in the past a good deal of practical work was performed, there exists a dearth of accumulated record. Hence no organised or scientific body of knowledge could be officially reared on the original skeletal framework of the traditional teaching.

Whatever the nature of these criticisms, I must logically exclude from my strictures such capable initiates as Mathers, Westcott, Brodie-Innes, and one or two others. But the present-day Chiefs have been so ashamed secretly of their lack of ability, and their absence of magical initiative and pioneering spirit, as well as of the puerility of their intellectual outlook in connection with the traditional technique, that they engineered unconsciously a revenge upon the Order. As compensation for their own futility, for their own psychic and spiritual deficiencies, they have foisted upon the whole Order the paucity of their own attainment. They have projected their inferiority upon their subordinates by refusing to acknowledge any intelligence either past or present keener than their own. In the presence of practical work suggesting initiative or the experimental spirit they have responded solely with cheap sneers and cynicisms. Under the hypocritical and, in my estimation, dogmatic guise of scepticism which was cultivated ostensibly to protect students from the dangers of dogma, they have with-held every scrap of useful material having an experimental origin and which might be serviceable as establishing valid and primary principles of Magical practice. Each student, therefore, is required by this attitude to commence anew investigations into the unknown world of the psyche, working completely in the dark as to what his predecessors and immediate colleagues may have accomplished or proved. Years of effort are thus unnecessarily wasted in

114

discovering fundamental principles of successful Magic—years which easily could have been saved. Consider the long and arduous labour which might have been more fruitfully expended in entirely new directions if ordinary commonsense and scientific procedures had been observed. What could not have been accomplished?

For this reason also is it that we find the strange anomaly of a Frater of ten or more years standing enquiring, in a letter addressed to the present writer: "What is the factor that master-magicians took for granted, and therefore saw no need of describing, that we omit?" The truth is not that these factors were never recorded. They were, and study reveals their presence in certain of the more important documents. But these latter were never stressed; in fact, were suppressed. And experiments based upon their principia were far from encouraged, while those that were undertaken were as soon forgotten. This, to the detriment of the Order itself as an experimental institution, and the system which it was supposed to espouse.

Another interesting side-light which illustrates the haphazard manner in which habitually the work was done, concerns this same matter of talismans. For reasons given above, this was one of the subjects which intrigued me enormously. It seemed to me capable of far-reaching developments. During the winter of 1933-34 circumstances enabled me to carry out a good deal of experimental work in connection with the charging of different kinds of talismans and flashing tablets for various ends. A certain, though very limited, success was obtained in that technique, I believe—that is if the high testimony of the Chiefs may be accepted, since the talismans in some instances were subjected to their tests. In conversation with one of them, in the fervent hope that perhaps some help might be given which would improve my technique, from her lips these words fell, though hardly as pearls of wisdom. "When you come to the talisman examination you should have very little difficulty. The regulations call for charging two or three talismans, and you should easily be able to do these."

But examinations were not my major interest. Such a concern would be futile and fatuous. It was the subject of talismans and flashing tablets in which I then had concern, to discover whether or no they were chargeable, and whether they were capable of producing spiritual or objective results. The above remark practically sums up the offiicial attitude to magical and mystical processes. The sole objective was not the absolute mastery of the magical technique, but simply the assumption of still more grades. It seems that in any of the subjects described in the official programme a bare minimum of work was required, and no more, to pass an examination—and that no conclusive one either. The nature of the tests themselves was utterly inconclusive and superficial, indicating absolutely nothing. In about three months the writer had successfuly passed almost two-thirds of the examinations required of the theoretical five years' work of the Adeptus Minor.

The lifting of the veil of life and penetrating to the spiritual aspects underlying it, demands not the petty attitude described above, but, as Jung puts it, "the most thoroughgoing and wearisome preparation, consisting in the right payment of all debts to life. For as long as one is in any way held by the domination of *cupiditas,* the veil is not lifted, and the heights of a consciousness empty of content and free of illusion are not reached, *nor can any trick nor any deceit bring it about."*

Another highly important phase of Magic consists of the personal application of the practical formulae drawn from the Neophyte ritual. From these formulae are compiled rituals for the invocation, for example, of the higher and divine Genius, the most important of all magical works. Other tasks which are assisted by these magical

116

formulae concern operations for the evocation of planetary and elemental spirits, the full formulae of consecration, the art of attaining invisibility and transformation, as well as an elaborate technique for ceremonial divination and alchemy.

For one thing, the document explaining these formula was almost wholly suppressed. Then a revised version was issued, in which fully half of the original material had been deleted. And in the very last letter I had from the Imperator, it was proposed to garble it still further—with which decision, just prior to my resignation, I expressed my absolute disagreement. Its contents were not in the last understood—the suppression implies that—because there had been no technical application of its principles. At one time, the attainment of the grade of Adeptus Major demanded the preparation of a complete ceremony based upon these formulae for any purpose that appealed to the examinee. Naturally, the ability to operate these technical methods successfully so as to produce the results desired, demanded a considerable amount of preliminary rehearsal and study and practical experience. This, it would seem, did not appeal to those who were consumed by the lust for grades, and so the document was eliminated after first having been labelled "unofficial." The Chiefs themselves, so they informed me, had *once* performed *one* of these ceremonies—but only, however, as one might have anticipated, to pass an examination!

How mastery of any technique can be acquired by a single application of a complex formula is a conclusion whose logic somewhat escapes my comprehension. If the operations mean anything at all, and it is my profound conviction that they do, then ceremony after ceremony must be performed, implying prolonged experiment, to acquire such skill. The effort to disclose the essence of mind or to exalt one's spiritual nature, requires a thorough-going analysis and intense labour extended over a period of many years, not merely a childish and superficial respect for conventional forms. The road to Adeptship is not a parlour game. It is a serious, tremendously difficult and arduous journey, of life-long duration.

My attitude to this, as to most other forms of Magic upon which both tradition and modern experience have placed the burden of true attainment, is, looking at the matter from another point of view, that a single operation means absolutely nothing either as a discipline towards self-development or as yielding scientific evidence as to the effectualness of the method employed. A single performance on the part of each of twenty individuals has little evidential value and can indicate nothing as to whether or not the formula is effectual. A dozen operations however undertaken, let us assume, by each of three or four individuals, may yield a significant body of evidence from which one may legitimately deduce whether the system or formula is of spiritual or developmental value.

By this special and persistent type of magical activity the powers of the soul will eventually have been so developed and stimulated that the actual external ceremonial can then be dispensed with. Then also the spiritual pilgrimage may proceed interiorly without the props and aids which this training does afford. Let it be admitted that Magic is an artificial system of props and aids. It is as such principally of value to the beginner in that it disposes towards or confirms a habit of will, aspiration or mental concentration. It produces these as few other systems of props or aids is able to. These artifices may be discarded when the exigencies of preliminary training have been fulfilled. Yet for this very reason it is totally erroneous with but an occasional exception to eliminate that training before skill has been acquired. In a sense, therefore, my own viewpoint is in accord with certain individuals in the modern Temple who have held that as

118

the initiate proceeds upon his way the more elaborate and complex forms of Ceremonial become unnecessary. But as against this, it is abundantly clear that there are very few here in the West whose spiritual capacity is so great that they are capable of running before they can walk. These ceremonial methods teach the aspirant to walk magically, and from experience with them he may learn how to run. The technique is for the beginner. And there is no shame to admit this. For in the path towards the ineffable Light, and in spiritual things generally, most of us are beginners. We therefore cannot possibly afford to dispense with the little artifices and conventions which provide the necessary discipline, thus stimulating the spiritual power, to assist our onward progress.

CHAPTER FIVE

LIGHT IN EXTENSION

Having said so much in criticism of the Order of the Golden Dawn and its system, my present task now is done. A thankless task it has been. A work encompassed by innumerable difficulties and obstacles. By many months of rigid self-examination and brooding over the advisability of this venture has it been preceded. Almost a year has elapsed since I first discussed with other individuals my instinct that this disclosure was necessary. Knowing what I do of the Golden Dawn members, and remembering the horrible rumours that years ago were deliberately circulated about Crowley, I must expect and am prepared for a flood of abuse and recrimination. What here has been said of the Hermetic Order of the Golden Dawn may apply equally well to a vast number of other so-called occult bodies which have far less foundation beneath them than the Golden Dawn. They also will be highly incensed by my "giving the show away." But Magic and Mysticism do not comprise for me a show. They are entirely too sacred and I feel too keenly on their behalf quietly to sit back and watch dissension and the menacing process of disintegration and corruption have free access to a stately system. Rather would it be wiser to destroy that tendency to desecration, and give the teaching itself to those to whom it belongs by right of spiritual inheritance—to all men and women everywhere in quest of the Light.

A torrent of malicious slander was let loose after the publication of my *Tree of Life*, and quite wrongfully I was calumniated, vilified and slandered. And for no adequate reason that I can see. No obligations were broken, and certainly no smirch was reflected upon the divine Theurgy which to me was, and still is, the only thing worth while in life and living. Even more calumny may be released by the issue of this preliminary publication, like black qliphotic ravens with vilification beneath their wings. But that is not my concern. Herein, and in my subsequent book *The Golden Dawn*, has only been done what I have considered to be my duty, even if it has entailed the breaking of an obligation—even if eventually it does entail the destruction of the present Temples. But the destruction or death of the Order is not necessarily a thing of evil in itself. Occasionally death may be a welcome event. "This is my body which I destroy in order that it may be renewed." Destruction may be necessary at times in order that from the ruins a more lasting, and permanent and beautiful construction may be raised. Great good may sometimes issue phoenix like, from the depths of the tomb. And the Order teaching itself may well imply that death, or apparent destruction by the typhonic forces, is necessary to the being not only of godhead but to all things which are the vehicles of godhead—organisations and societies included. "Buried with that Light in a mystical death, rising again in a mystical resurrection, cleansed and purified . . . ." From the pastos, from the dark grave, from the destruction which may perhaps come to the Hermetic Order of the Golden Dawn or its offspring the Stella Matutina, let there arise a new and more golden splendour which, cleansed and purified by its abeyance, may prove itself a more worthy vehicle of the divine teaching of the archaic search for the Light, to bring the glory of the stars to the hearts of men.

Thus my motives should be perfectly clear. In this small work and its sequel *The Golden Dawn* nothing has been kept back. Without reserve have I deliberately revealed as under a surgeon's scalpel the rotting tissues which have clogged the pulsating heart of the hidden knowledge. May the publication of that inner heart be as the removal of that rot and disintegrating process which has attacked the Order and threatened the vitality of its magical system. Despite the condemnation and criticism I have considered so urgent and necessary, it should be evident to all that I have only the deepest respect and love and veneration for the sacred cause which the Golden Dawn espoused. Its teaching and its ceremonial system thrill me intensely and have evoked deep admiration within me. It is now many years since first the distant echo of its music reached my ear. It came to me through the reading of strange and forbidding literatures and by devious ways in a distant land. And in those many years I have journeyed far, physically as well as spiritually, in quest of that light and music. Alas, when finally I was able to find it, the light had been dimmed by an ugly shroud, and the music of that lofty rite was marred by an evil discord. Let me therefore assure the public that this violation of obligation that knowingly I have taken upon myself has been for the primary object of placing before all that same light I then envisaged, that music so faintly heard, by attempting to remove as best I might that shroud and banishing that cacophony. This I have done to save other people if at all possible the journey and the unnecessarily difficult labours which beset my own quest for the Light. I am not an enemy of the Golden Dawn. Certainly not of Magic. But I shall always most emphatically decry any attempt to whittle away the magical tradition. We have seen what fate overtook the Theosophical Society when a concerted effort was made to whittle away the Secret Doctrine. And I shall always reject a magical popery, or any attempt to exploit within the Order or in the Name of Magic any weaker members or to abuse and despoil the ineffable rites. More than aught else it is this latter which arouses me violently to

122

anger.

This statement of the Golden Dawn secret knowledge may perhaps be comparable to the appearance, in another field, of *The Mahatma Letters* edited by Mr. A. Trevor Barker. I mention this that condemnation of my apparent treachery, justifiable at first sight, may be silenced and my action seen in its true light. In those letters was the injunction that they should not be published. But the state of the Theosophical movement induced Mr. Barker to edit those letters and produce a volume which since has been welcomed by many hundreds of people. At the time, however, he was roundly abused for his brave gesture. I have heard such abuse issuing from members of an association whose Theosophical orthodoxy cannot be questioned. Posterity may yet conclude that his timely volume saved that movement. In my estimation, true magical teaching is no whit less important than Theosophy, and that the foundation of the Golden Dawn though less spectacular was certainly as significant in the history of spiritual progress as the Theosophical Society. The fate of the one was the same fate that befell the other. The corruptions that threatened Theosophy also occurred to the divine Theurgy taught in the Golden Dawn. And the letters of the Mahatmas in which the true Theosophy can be found must be considered as a definite statement of what Thesophy is, just as the veridic teachings of the age-old Theurgy may be found in the original unexpurgated documents circulated in the Golden Dawn. This teaching is the true Theurgy, not the inane burblings and private opinions of those who perpetually prate of the sanctity of Order obligations.

So far from wishing to betray or profane the Order, it is my sincerest wish that by this publication it may be considerably aided. May this work and its sequel arouse, on the part of general readers, a keener desire than ever before for occult knowledge of a trustworthy nature.

123

Some of these may feel that personal instruction and guidance is still necessary. Though the instructions to be reprinted in *The Golden Dawn* are ample to guide the intelligent and sincere student—it is all the instruction that a good many of us got, despite the frequent assertions as to the existence of an oral tradition—yet here again and for these people the Order may fulfil the high purpose of its foundation. If it will cleanse itself from within, and eliminate those elements or individuals or tendencies whose presence is inimical to the progress and welfare of the Order, then it may look forward to a healthy and happy future. In it Magic may still find its champion—a sanctuary where the true processes may even now be taught.

Yet as said above, I consider the documents which will appear in my forthcoming book, sufficient to guide any individual of ordinary intelligence and insight and aspiration. So long as he pays strict attention to every statement made, and truly studies the entire system with great care, exercising both common sense and intuitive perception, no outside help should be required for quite a long time. When then he really requires it, his very efforts to have applied the technique will automatically cause that assistance to gravitate towards him.

One final word about the Obligations. They were very solemn and serious oaths that were demanded in the *Golden Dawn,* and were imposed under the most dramatic circumstances conceivable. The candidate either knelt before the altar with his hand on a sacred symbol and the other held in that of the Chief, as in the Neophyte ceremony, or else, as in the Adeptus Minor grade, he was bound to a Cross. In the latter, as previously described, an Angelic force was invoked to bear witness that an oath had been taken, and to demand vengeance were that vow broken. I am not unmindful of the solemnity of this oath, nor of this latter penalty clause. Were there no other reasons for hesitation concerning this scheme, then this one at least would have been quite sufficient to have given me pause, to induce long and pained reflection. Should there actually be occult powers behind the Order as seriously is claimed, then it is my conviction that those forces —whether they be conceived of as Adepts and Masters, or even Angelic in nature—can hardly be delighted with the undignified occurrences of the past several years. It is a truism in occult circles as a whole that if a recalcitrant member of a genuine occult brotherhood breaks his oath, an avenging punitive current comes automatically into operation, though his defection may have passed totally unnoticed by the visible chiefs of his Temple. On the other hand, also, if the Frater or member is in the true spirit of the tradition and cares more for the welfare of that tradition than do his chiefs, the power invoked in the obligation may manifest itself as a mighty protective influence with which the Chiefs themselves will collide.

Hence, there is little that need unduly concern me. If I have wronged the Order, its guardians will know how and where and in what way I may be punished. If I am guilty of treachery and have mistakenly worked against the intent and purpose of the true occult forces behind the Golden Dawn, those intelligent powers concerned with the initiation of mankind, then willingly I open myself to the avenging punitive current. On the other hand, there is little doubt but that I may expect every assistance in this my venture of publication should those guardians also feel that the Order has finished its day. Herein and deliberately, by this very act, do I, Ad Majorem Adonai Gloriam, Zelator Adeptus Minor R.R. et A.C., invoke that same guardian of the Mysteries before whom I sincerely swore, when bound on the Cross of Obligation, that I would devote myself to the Great Work, and that always and at all times shall I have the best interests of that work at heart. And if I fail herein, and if my present

125

act be contrary to the true intent of whatever divine powers may be, willingly let my "Rose be blasted and my power in Magic cease."

Let me now detail the curriculum of work prescribed in the Second Order. The training of the Adeptum Minor consists of eight separate items, and I quote the following from a syllabus "A—General Orders," now in circulation.

"*Part One. A. Preliminary.* Receive and copy: Notes on the Obligation. The Ritual of the ⑤ = ⑥ Grade. The manuscript, Sigils from the Rose. The Minutum Mundum. Having made your copies of these and returned the originals you should study them in order to prepare to sit for the written examination. You must also arrange with the Adept in whose charge you are, about your examination in the Temple on the practical work."

It will be well for the reader to note the wording of the above. It may have been thought that my remarks in a former chapter on the perverseness of the Order examination system were rather severe or unjust. Or that perhaps I had exaggerated the matter. But if the above paragraph is read attentively, the whole matter is made clear and my description is given corroboration. It perfectly describes the official attitude. "You should study the papers" not in order to master the matters described nor to benefit by the material, but only "in order to prepare to sit for the written examination." This puerile and unintelligent spirit pervaded every department of the Order and forced its way insidiously and secretly into the mental outlook of almost all who passed through its portals.

"*Part Two.* Receive the Rituals of the Pentagram and Hexagram. Copy and learn them. You can now sit for the written examination in these subjects and complete 'A' by arranging to be tested in your practical knowledge in the Temple.

"*Part One. B. Implements.* Receive the Rituals of the

Lotus Wand, Rose-Cross, Sword, and the Elemental Weapons. Copy and return them. There is a written examination on the above subjects—that is on the construction, symbolism, and use of these objects, and the general nature of a consecration ceremony and the forming of invocations. This can be taken before the practical work of making is begun or at any stage during it.

"*Part Two.* This consists in the making of the Implements which must be passed as suitable before the consecration is arranged for, in the presence of a Chief or other qualified Adept. The making and consecration are done in the order given above unless it is preferred to do all the practical work first, and make arrangements for consecration as convenient.

"*Part One. G. Neophyte Formulae.* Receive and copy Z.I. on the symbols and formulae of the Neophyte Ritual. Z.3. the symbolism of Neophyte in this Ceremony. Copy the God-form designs of the Neophyte Ritual. The written examination on the Z. manuscripts may now be taken.

"*Part Two.* To describe to the Chief or other suitable Adept in the Temple the arrangement of the Astral Temple and the relative positions of the Forms in it. To build up any God-form required, using the correct Coptic Name."

The above three sections, A. B. G., completed the course prescribed for the Zelator Adeptus Minor, the first sub-grade. The passing of these examinations conferred the qualification for holding the office of Hierophant in the Outer Order of the G.D.

"*Part One. C. Psychic.* This consists in a written examination in the Tatwa system. Its method of use, and an account of any one vision you have had from any card.

"*Part Two.* This consists in making a set of Tatwa

cards, if you have not already done so, and sending them to be passed by the Chief or other Adept appointed. To take the examiner on a Tatwic journey, instructing him as if he were a student and vibrating the proper names for a selected symbol.

"*Part One. D. Divination.* Receive and study the Tarot system, making notes of the principal attributions of the Inner method.

"*Part Two. Practical.* On a selected question, either your own, or the examiner's, to work out a Divination first by Geomancy, then by Horary Astrology, then by the complete Inner Tarot system, and send in a correlated account of the result.

"*Part One. F. Angelic Tablets.* Receive and make copies of the Enochian Tables, the Ritual of the Concourse of the Forces, and the Ritual of the making of the Pyramids, Sphinx, and God-form for any square. A written examination on these subjects may now be taken.

"*Part Two.* Make and colour a pyramid for a selected square, and to make the God-form and Sphinx suitable to it, and to have this passed by an Adept. To prepare a Ritual for practical use with this square, and in the presence of a Chief or other Adept appointed to build it up astrally and describe the vision produced. To study and play Enochian chess, and to make one of the Chess boards and a set of Chessmen.

"*Part One. E. Talismans.* Receive a manuscript on the making and consecrating of Talismans. Gather Names, Sigils, etc., for a Talisman for a special purpose. Make a design for both designs of it and send it in for a Chief to pass. Make up a special ritual for consecrating to the purpose you have in mind and arrange a time with the Chief for the Ceremony of Consecration."

"This completes the work of a Theoricus Adeptus Minor."

In a corresponding document, setting forth the curriculum as it is followed in another Temple, and I have checked this with yet a third document dated 1894, it is clear that an important item has been eliminated from the manuscript which I have quoted. I give it below:

"H. *Consecration and Evocation. Subject*: A ceremony on the formulae of Ritual Z.2. Must be prepared before Examiner and must meet with his approval as to method, execution and effect."

In the early Temples there was also issued a catalogue of manuscripts, enumerating in alphabetical order the documents circulated amongst the Zelatores Adepti Minores.

A. General Orders. The Curriculum of Work prescribed.

B. The Lesser and Supreme Ritual of the Pentagram.

C. The Rituals of the Hexagram.

D. Description of Lotus Wand, and Ritual Consecration.

E. Description of Rose Cross and the Ritual of Consecration.

F. Sigils from the Rose.

G. Sword and Four Implements, with Consecration ritual.

H. Clavicula Tabularum Enochi.

J. Notes on the Obligation of the Adeptus Minor.

K. Consecration Ceremony of the Vault. L. History Lecture.

M. Hermes Vision, and Lineal Figures of the Sephiroth.

N.O.P.Q.R. Complete Treatise on the Tarot, with Star Maps.

S. The Attributions of the Enochian Tablets.

T. The Book of The Angelical Keys or Calls.

U. Lecture on Man, the Microcosm.

W. Hodos Chamelionis, the Minutum Mundum.

X. The Egyptian God-forms as applied to the Enochian Squares.

Y. Enochian Chess.

Z. Symbolism of the Temple, Neophyte, and Ritual of the 0-0 grade.

All the documents from A to Z listed above will be found reproduced in my forthcoming book *The Golden Dawn,* though I have not retained that particular order. The sole omissions are the documents lettered H., J., L. and part of M.

"J" consists simply of an elaborate commentary upon the Adeptus Minor Obligation, written in a florid ponderous style, reminiscent of Eliphas Levi-cum-Arthur Edward Waite.

"H" Clavicula Tabularum Enochi, is a more or less lengthy manuscript, turgid and archaic, for the most part repeating, though not as clearly, the contents of "S, The Book of the Concourse of the Forces." Incidentally, this document is practically a verbatim duplicate of part of a lengthy manuscript to be found in the Manuscript Library of the British Museum, Sloane 307. A good deal of the advice given is typically mediaeval, and definitely unsound from a spiritual viewpoint, and is certainly not in accord with the general lofty tenor of the remaining Order teaching. It explains how to find precious metals and hidden treasure, and how to drive away the elemental guardians thereof. It is an inferior piece of work—as also is the document "L", and so I have decided to omit both.

"M" has two sections, the Hermes Vision which I do propose to give, and the Lineal Figures of the Sephiroth. Because of the extreme complexity of the latter, and because it will be impossible to reproduce the several drawings in colour which accompany that manuscript, the writer has deemed it sufficient to restate it in a general manner as a note to the instruction on Telesmatic Images.

Clearly, from these disclosures there may be drastic results. But the good, I trust, will immeasurably and ultimately outweigh whatever evil may come. That some careless people will hurt themselves and burn their fingers experimenting with matters not wholly understood seems almost inevitable. Theirs, however, will be the fault. For the formulae of Magic require intensive study prior to experimental work. And since all the important formulae are to be given in their entirety, and nothing withheld that is of the least value, there should be no excuse for anybody harming himself. No serious hurt should come to anyone. On the contrary, the gain to those serious students of Magic and Mysticism who have initiative and yet refuse to involve themselves with corrupt occult orders, and it is to these that I fain would speak, should be immeasurable.

You are being given a complete system of attainment. This you must study and develop at your own leisure, applying it in your own particular way. The system is complete and effectual, as well as noble. The grade rituals as I shall reproduce them have been tampered with, in some cases unintelligently. Their efficacy, however, is not impaired, for the principal portion of those grade rituals, which teaches the art of invocation, is intact. So that the unwise editing that they have received in the past several years, has not actually damaged them; all that has been removed are a few items, more or less unimportant, of Qabalistic knowledge. If the reader feels that these might be of value to him, and for the sake of tolerable completeness would like to have them, by studying such Qabalistic texts as the *Zohar* and the *Sepher Yetzirah*, both of which are now in English translation, or some such work as Waite's *Holy Kaballah*, he will be in possession of the fundamental facts. It is in other parts of the Order work that injudicious tampering has been at work. Most of this is now restored and I believe that my future book *The Golden Dawn* will represent the whole of the Order work from Neophyte to Theoricus Adeptus Minor.

Some portions of the manuscripts have required editing, principally from the literary point of view. Whole paragraphs have had to be deleted, others shortened, sentences made more clear, the redundant use of many words eliminated, and a general coordination of the manuscripts undertaken. Certain other sections—those dealing at length with Talismans, Sigils, Clairvoyance, Geomancy, and the Enochian Tablets—have been completely rewritten to render them more coherent. But nothing that is essential or vital to the magical tenor or understanding of any document will be omitted, changed or altered. This I avow and publicly swear. Where personally I have seen fit to make comment on any matter in order to clarify the issue or to indicate its antecedents, or connections in other parts of the work, that comment or remark is so marked by me with initials.

Let me therefore urge upon the sincere reader whose wish it is to study this magical system, to pay great attention to the scheme of the grade rituals, to obtain a bird's eye view of the whole, to study every point, its movement and teaching. This should be repeated again and again, until the mind moves easily from one point of the ritual to another. The synthetic outline of those rituals presented in Chapter Two of this book should be found helpful as assisting in this task. Let him also study the diagrams of the Temple lay-out, and build up in his imagination a clear and vivid picture of that Temple together with the appropriate officers and their movements. Then it will be an easy matter to devise a simple form of self-initiation. It will be simple to adapt the text to solo performance. But a careful scrutiny and examination of the entire system should long precede any effort to do practical work, if serious harm and danger is to be avoided. The language needs to be mastered, and the symbolic ideas of the whole system assimilated and incorporated into the very fibre of one's being. Intellectual acquaintance with every aspect of the subject is just as necessary as personal integrity and selfless devotion to an ideal. Sincerity is indeed the most trustworthy shield and buckler that any student may possess, but if he neglects the intellectual mastery of the subject, he will soon discover where his heel of Achilles is located. But these two combined are the only safeguards, the fundamental requisites to an insight into the significance of Magic. Not only are they the only sure foundation, but they conduce to the continual recollection of the goal at the end. This understanding arises through penetrating to the root of the matter, without which the student may stray but too readily from the narrow way stretching before him. No matter how brilliant his intellectual capacity, no matter how ardent his sincerity or potent his dormant magical power, always must he remember that they matter absolutely in no way unless applied to the Great Work—the knowledge and conversation of the Higher and Divine Genius. "Power without wisdom," said a poet, "is the name of Death." And as Frater D.D.C.F. so rightly said of one phase of magical work, but which has its application to the whole scheme, "Know thou that this is not to be done lightly for thine own amusement or experiment, seeing that the forces of Nature were not created to be thy plaything or toy. Unless thou doest thy practical magical works with solemnity, ceremony and reverence, thou shalt be like an infant playing with fire, and thou shalt bring destruction upon thyself." In deviation from these injunctions lie the only actual dangers in the divine science.

One of the essentials of preliminary work, is the committing to memory of the important correspondences and attributions. And I cannot insist too srongly that this is fundamental. The student must make himself familiar first of all with the Hebrew Alphabet, and learn how to write the names of the Sephiroth and Deity Names in that tongue—he will realise their value when he approaches the practical work of invocation. Much time should be spent studying and meditating upon the glyph of the Tree of Life and memorising all the important attributions—divine Names, names of Archangels, Angels and Spheres and elements. All the symbols referred to the lamens of the officers should be carefully meditated upon, as also the various admission badges, and other symbols given in the knowledge lectures.

The student can easily adapt any fair-sized room to the exigencies of a Temple. The writer has worked in one hardly larger than a long cupboard, about ten feet long by six or seven wide. All furniture from the centre should be cleared away, leaving a central space in which he may freely move and work. A small table covered with a black cloth will suffice for the Altar, and the two Pillars may be dispensed with but formulated in the imagination as present. He may find it very useful to paint flashing Angelic Tablets according to the instructions found elsewhere, as well as the Banners of the East and West, placing these in the appropriate cardinal quarters of his improvised Temple. If he is able to obtain small plaster-casts, bull and man—and place these in the proper stations, they will be found together with the Tablets to impart a considerable amount of magical vitality and atmosphere to the Temple. What actually they do bestow is rather subtle, and perhaps indefinable. They are not absolute essentials, however, and may be dispensed with. But since Magic works by the intervention of symbol and emblem, the surrounding of the student's sphere with the correct forms of magical symbolism, assists in the impressing of these symbols within the aura or sphere of sensation, the true magical Temple. This may be left to the ingenium and the convenience of the student himself to discover after having made a close examination of the documents involved.

Another matter upon which brief comment must be made concerns the Instruments. It would have given me great pleasure to have had illustrations of these reproduced in colour, for only thus can one appreciate their significance and the part they play in ceremonial. But this unfortunately may not be possible. Thus they will probably be given only in black and white, which obviously cannot impart anything but the merest fraction of their actual beauty and suggestiveness. And I impress upon the serious student, even implore him, to betake upon himself the trouble of making these instruments himself. They are very simple to fashion. And the results obtained, to say little of the knowledge acquired or the intuitive processes that somehow are stimulated by that effort, are well worth even a great deal of bother. To adopt temporarily part of the terminology now current among analytical psychologists, and identify the latent spiritual self of man with what is known as the Unconscious, then be it remembered that this vast subterranean stream of vitality and memory and inspiration can only be reached by means of a symbol. For the latter, states Jung, "is the primitive expression of the Unconscious, while on the other hand it is an idea corresponding to the highest intuition produced by consciousness." Thus these weapons and magical instruments are symbolic representation of psychic events, of forces inhering within the potentiality of the inner man. By means of their personal manufacture, magical consecration and continual employment they may be made to affect and stimulate the dormant side of man's nature. It is an interesting fact that in his practice, Jung encouraged his patients to paint symbolic designs which sometimes were comparable to the Eastern mandals. It seems that the effort to paint these designs had the effect of straightening out stresses and knots in the unconscious, thus accomplishing the therapeutic object of analysis. And not only were they thus means of self-expression but these designs produced a counter-effect of fascinating, healing and stimulating to renewed activity the hitherto unmanifested psyche.

With the exception that the ordinary magical student is not neurotic or psychopathic, the techniques are rather similar. For the magical tradition has always insisted upon the routine to be followed by the aspirant to that art. He was required to fashion the implements himself, and the more laborious he found that task, with the greater difficulties thrown before him, by so much more were those efforts of spiritual value. For not only are these instruments symbols or expressions of inner realities, but what is infinitely more of practical worth, their actual projection in this way from within outwards, the physical fashioning and painting of these instruments also works an effect. They bring to life the man that was asleep. They react upon their maker. They become powerful magical agents, true talismans of power.

Thus, the Lotus Wand is declared in the Ritual to have the colours of the twelve signs of the Zodiac painted on its stem, and it is surmounted by the Lotus flower of Isis. It symbolises the development of creation. The Wand has

136

ever been a symbol of the magical Will, the power of the spirit in action. And its description in the instruction on the Lotus Wand is such that it is seen to embrace the whole of Nature—the Sephiroth, the spiritual aspects of the elements, and the action of the Sun upon all life by a differentiating process. Even as the whole of nature is the embodiment of a dynamic will, the visible form and vehicle of a spiritual consciousness. The Lotus flower grows from the darkness and gloom of the secret depths, through the waters, ever striving to open its blossoms on the surface of the waters to the rays and light of the Sun. So is the true magical or spiritual will secreted within the hidden depths of the soul of man. Unseen, sometimes unknown and unsuspected, it lies latent through the whole of the life. By these rites of Magic, its symbols and exercises, we are enabled to assist its growth and development, by piercing through the outer husks of the restricting shell, until it bursts into full bloom—the flower of the human spirit, the Lotus of the higher Soul. "Look for the flower to bloom in the silence . . . It shall grow, it will shoot up, it will make branches and leaves and form buds while the storm continues, while the battle lasts . . . It is the flower of the Soul that has opened." Note, moreover, the description of and the comment made by Jung to a symbolic design brought to him by one of his patients, evidently a design like to the Lotus Wand, for he says: "The plant is frequently a structure in brilliant fiery colours and is shown growing out of a bed of darkness and carrying the blossom of light at the top, a symbol similar to the Christmas tree." This is highly suggestive, and students both of Yoga and Magic will find in this curious indications of the universality of symbols. Magical processes and symbols are, in short, receiving confirmation at the hands of experimental psychology. It remains for the reader to benefit thereby.

The Rose-Cross is a Lamen or badge synthesising a

vast concourse of ideas, representing in a single emblem the Great Work itself—the harmonious reconciliation in one symbol of diverse and apparently contradictory concepts, the reconciliation of divinity and manhood. It is a highly important symbol to be worn over the heart during every important operation. It is a glyph, in one sense, of the higher Genius to whose knowledge and conversation the student is eternally aspiring. In the Rituals it is described as the Key of Sigils and Rituals.

The Sword is a weapon symbolizing the critical dispersive faculty of the mind. It is used where force and strength are required, more particularly for banishing than for invoking—as though conscious intellection were allied to the power of Will. When employed in certain magical ceremonies with the point upwards, its nature is transformed into an instrument similar to the Wand. The Elemental weapons of the Wand, Cup, Dagger, and Pentacle are symbolical representations of the forces employed for the manifestation of the inner self, the elements required for the incarnation of the divine. They are attributed to the four letters of Tetragrammaton. All of these are worth making, and by creating them and continually employing them intelligently in the ways shown by the various rituals, the student will find a new power developing within him, a new centre of life building itself up from within.

One last word of caution. Let me warn the student against attempting difficult and complex ceremonies before he has mastered the more simple ones. The syllabus provided on a former page for the use of the Minor Adept grades the work rather well. The consecration ceremonies for the magical implements are, of their kind, excellent examples of ceremonial work. Classical in nature, they are simple in structure and operation, and provide a harmonious and easily flowing ritual. A good deal of experience should be obtained with the constant use of these and similar types which the student should himself construct along these lines. A variety of things may occur to his mind for which a variety of operations may be performed. This of course, applies only to that phase of his studies when then preliminary correspondence and attributions have been thoroughly memorised and what is more, understood, and when the meditations have been performed. This likewise is another matter upon which too much emphasis cannot be laid.

Above all, the Pentagram and Hexagram rituals should be committed to memory so that no effort is required to recall at a moment's notice the points or angles of these figures from which the invocation of a certain force commences. Short ceremonies should be devised having as their object the frequent use of these lineal figures so that they become a part of the very manner in which the mind works during ceremonial. After some time has elapsed, and after considerable experience with the simple consecration formulae, and the student feels more confident of himself and his ritualistic capacity, let him turn to the more complex ceremonies whose formulae are summarised in the manuscript Z. 2. These require much preparation, intensive study, and a great deal of rehearsal and experience. Moreover, he must not be disappointed if, at first, the results fall short of his anticipations. Persistence is an admirable and necessary virtue, particularly in Magic. And let him endeavour to penetrate into the reasons for the apparent worthlessness or puerility of the aims of these formulae, such as transformation, evocation, invisibility, by reflection on the spiritual forces which must flow through him in order to effect such ends. And let him beware of the booby trap which was set up in the Order—of doing but one of these ceremonies, or superficially employing any phase of the system as though to pass an examination, and considering in consequence, that he is master of the technique.

My work is done.

"Let us work, therefore, my brethren and effect right-
eousness, because the Night cometh when no man shall
labour . . . . May the Light which is behind the veil
shine through you from your throne in the East on the
Fratres and Sorores of the Order and lead them to perfect
day, when the glory of this world passes and a great light
shines over the splendid sea."

Valeté Fratres et Sorores.

Roseae Rubeae et Aureae Crucis. Benedictus Dominus
deus noster qui dedit nobis Signum.

Ex Deo Nascimur. In Yeheshuah Morimur. Revivi-
scimus per Spiritus Sanctus.

London
February, 1935.

CHAPTER SIX

SOME MODERN CRITICS

Apparently the peroration to the body of the original text of this book was premature. It seems as if my work with the Golden Dawn itself or with Aleister Crowley were not wholly finished—unfortunately. I often wish it were. But since the past does not totally die, nor the dead remain buried, some of the controversial issues raised in *My Rosicrucian Adventure* seem to surface periodically.

Three books referred to earlier need to be dealt with, not at great length however, but enough to complete certain themes. Their titles are:

The Unicorn by Virginia Moore (MacMillan Co., N.Y. 1954)

The Inner Teachings of the Golden Dawn by R.G. Torrens, B.A. (Neville Spearman, London, 1969)

Ritual Magic in England (American edition entitled *Secret Rites of Occult Magic*) by Francis King (MacMillan Co., N.Y., 1971)

If the student will have read the main body of the text before he arrives at this postscript, he will clearly understand the necessity of these considerations.

Virginia Moore's *The Unicorn* is a fine piece of literary work. It grew originally out of her interest in William B. Yeats, and though many other biographies have been written about this Irish poet, hers is entirely different because she gained access to all sorts of fascinating information never previously dealt with. And above all, she investigated his alleged connections with the Golden

Dawn. Her persistence and thoroughness resulted in an elucidation of some post ⁻revolt events with which I was only remotely familiar. For this clarification of events I am most grateful. However, I am forced reluctantly to differ from some of her conclusions as previously explained at some length in my biographical study of Aleister Crowley, *The Eye in The Triangle*. Virginia Moore's devotion to Yeats and her undisguised hostility to Crowley has led her into several bogs—but these are of secondary importance.

It was she who first elucidated with some fine detail the connections of Dr. Felkin with Rudolph Steiner, which was a rather ironic impasse for Golden Dawn initiates to be brought to. The psychic intoxications of astral vision are well described, indicating the spiritual bankruptcy that had overtaken some of the branches and many of the members. Her book is strongly to be recommended to those students who wish to keep a record of the checkered and tragic history of the Order. I am under the impression that this invaluable work is currently out of print. Perhaps with demands made by the general public as a result of these and other references another edition of it may eventually be issued.

Perhaps the saddest matter described in her book is Yeats' abandonment of the Golden Dawn system of magic and spiritual attainment to wallow in that semi-hysterical and dark underworld of seances and mediums. It is difficult for me to understand that once having known of this initiatory system, any other approach could be substituted—especially that of spiritualism. I suppose it indicates the basic spiritual insecurity that existed in Yeats before he was able to discover himself. "My soul wanders in darkness and seeks the Light of the hidden knowledge," so says the Kerux on behalf of the candidate in the Neophyte Ritual. Initiation apparently never brought that Light to William Butler Yeats.

Anyway, these are but secondary considerations and need not necessarily concern us here, since after all we are mostly interested in the historical sequence of events rather than in personalities.

The third of the three books mentioned is *Secret Rites of Occult Magic* by Francis King. This is by far more interesting than Virginia Moore's book. It amplifies some of her historical material, but goes much further, and King is far less interested in defending or rejecting any one individual than she is, but provides many more important and intimate pieces of historical information than anyone else to date. He obviously has also had access to hitherto private or concealed information, and so it must be considered a highly authoritative text. The book is very well written, richly documented, and is shot through and through with some sly humor.

One of the previously obscure items connected with the revolt within the Order was Mr. and Mrs. Horos. Francis King elaborates this situation at some length, providing an enormous amount of insight into the unsavory activities of this couple of degenerates. I agree with the author that this episode in the Golden Dawn was very important to the extent that it thoroughly demoralized the ordinary rank and file of membership. Many members divorced themselves from the Order at this time—altogether apart from the other conflictual elements comprising the revolt, described both here and in the writing of Virginia Moore.

There are some highly illuminating comments upon the activity of Mr. Arthur Edward Waite. Some of them were sorely needed, for almost everybody with but a few exceptions seemed to be afraid of him and his reputation, so handling him with kid gloves. I recall when my book *The Philosopher's Stone* was accepted by Rider and Company many years ago, the editor called upon me to delete a number of derogatory statements made about Waite relative to his vicious criticisms of Mrs. Atwood and her book on alchemy. Unfortunately, I acceded to this request. The offending remarks were removed. To this very day, I regret my action.

But King is wholly unafraid here and shows Waite up for what he was. I love particularly King's remark on page 96: "The ritual revisions had been carried out by Waite and it cannot be denied that the language used was exceedingly pompous and long-winded—or at least so it appears at the present day." This is still treating Waite too kindly; only Aleister Crowley has dealt firmly, with both satire and humor, with this pompous, turgid Roman Catholic masquerading in occult dress.

King also clarifies the relationship that came to exist between Brodie-Innes of a North England Temple and McGregor Mathers. I had come to suspect that ultimately a *rapprochement* of some sort was worked out to the satisfaction of both parties, but had been unable at the time to discover any factual evidence to point in that direction. This evidence however is presented in full by King in this book—which is one of the many items that makes his work so valuable. Another item, minor admittedly, is the information that Evelyn Underhill, the highly gifted and informed writer on Christian mysticism, and Charles Williams who wrote several novels which sometimes had occult themes, were both members of Waite's splinter Temple.

There is also the clarification of an event of some few years ago which had puzzled me no little. In the fall of 1966, some friends in England sent me clippings from *The Daily Telegraph* announcing the discovery on a beach in Sussex of a wooden box containing magical instruments and regalia. After a Miss Judith Hobson and her father discovered it, taking it to the police, no one seemed to connect these findings with the Golden Dawn.

The clipping from the same paper dated the next day changed the entire picture. *The Daily Telegraph* announced that "Mr. Francis King, 32, an accountant, of Notting Hill, saw the report describing the contents of the box...." and pointed out "that whoever had owned the garments was of some eminence in the Order (that is, of the Golden Dawn), because he had reached the seventh grade, as was shown on his 'scarf of grades'." The first clipping described a plaque on which were carved the Latin words "Ex Fide Fortis" (a motto meaning "Strong in the Faith"). Who Ex Fide Fortis was did not appear to be known at that time, or at least it was not so stated.

In his book, Francis King gives the answer to these somewhat perplexing problems. Ex Fide Fortis was the Latin motto selected in the Order by a Mrs. Tranchell Hayes, and when the Order went into more or less abeyance after the publication of the first volume of my book *The Golden Dawn*, she boxed her paraphernalia and buried it in a cliff-top garden on the south coast of England. "Thirty years later, in the autumn of 1966, the cliff crumbled away and the box containing these magical implements fell into the sea and was washed upon a beach, where they were found by some passing visitors."

Curiously enough, around 1931 or so I had met Mrs. Tranchell Hayes, whom I understood from various sources since, was one of Dion Fortune's magical mentors. She was, at that time, married to a psychiatrist who practiced in a mental hospital in, if I remember rightly, Worcester. Crowley had occasionally corresponded from France with an astrologer in London by the name of Gabriel Dee. She was a pretty shrewd woman, and while interested in Crowley's literary output, suffered from no delusions relative to Crowley himself. After I met Gabriel Dee and we became good friends, she introduced me soon to Mrs. Hayes. There must have been some half-dozen times when we were invited up to Worcester from London for dinner and a long evening of interesting conversation. Her psychiatrist husband, on one occasion, taught me hypnotism which I have since incorporated into my current professional armamentarium. I have thought fondly of both of the Hayes on many an occasion. It never occurred to me, or was in any way conveyed to me, that she would have been so profoundly affected by these so-called "revelations" of my writing.

Another completely fascinating set of events narrated by Mr. King is the connection between L. Ron Hubbard of Dianetics and Scientology fame, and Jack Parsons who conducted a Temple of the O∴T∴O∴ in Pasadena, California. Immediately after World War II, I had come to Los Angeles intent upon building a practice there, and though I had heard round-about rumors of the existence of this Temple, I gave it very wide berth. At that time I was pretty well disillusioned with Aleister Crowley and had no use for the Golden Dawn, having then decided, as it were, to "go it alone". In 1952, I became aware of the spate of publicity in all the local newspapers relative to Parsons' death, when the house on Orange Grove in Pasadena was blown up by an explosion in his basement laboratory. Much of the long accumulated muck and yellow journalism about Crowley was rehashed and a lot of irresponsible writing was disgorged by journalists who saw nothing but a lurid story. Naturally, there were some vague and indirect references to the Golden Dawn—but these counted for nothing. The entire incident made me feel rather complacent and pleased that for once I had stayed out of the mess by not affiliating with them or even looking them up.

I was around when Dianetics finally broke into the science fiction pulp magazines, and had the hilarious opportunity of watching several colleagues, who should have known better, decamp under the aegis of Hubbard, and live long enough to recognize their stupidity. Then I got to know Mr. Louis Culling, the author of *The Complete Curriculum of the G∴B∴G∴*, who was at that time a member of the Pasadena O∴T∴O∴ Temple. He looked me up in my office ostensibly to procure manipulation for some sacroiliac difficulty. Hubbard was living at the Orange Grove house during Culling's tenure there. Culling from time to time has given me insights resembling those that King has depicted in his book. The whole escapade makes for fascinating reading, and is an amusing commentary on the foibles of human nature in some of its aspects. It also highlights some of the sparks thrown off by the Golden Dawn at various times in its history.

In his final chapter "A Summing Up", Mr. King has this to say: "Much of the Golden Dawn system was not original for component parts of it can be found scattered through the occult writings of a thousand years of European history....In the last analysis it is quite unimportant whether the synthesizer was Mathers or someone else; the important thing is that those who have really worked at the system in all its aspects have found that it is effective, that it achieves what it sets out to achieve."

With this conclusion, I am fundamentally in complete accord. Nonetheless, since I dislike loose ends, I do feel it would be a highly important project to trace out the European history of the predecessors of thsi magical Order. If the references to a Fraulein Anna Sprengel are authentic, there is implied that there were German remnants of the 18th century Rosicrucian organizations still extant and operative in Europe. Branches and feelers from

146

these were put out from time to time—one resulted in the organization of the Golden Dawn in England. Archives must still exist somewhere in Europe giving the principal items of this history. Frater Paragranus of the Swiss O∴T∴O∴ has such a library, or archives, and in the future it is incumbent upon one of the younger men to engage in research to delve out some of these origins.

Another important necessity in this connection is a biography of McGregor Mathers. Since the Golden Dawn, in one way or another, has affected the whole trend of modern occultism, it is incumbent upon us to discover the nature and character of this strange man. Strictly speaking, the Golden Dawn *was* McGregor Mathers. He was the Golden Dawn in very much the same way the Madame Blavatsky *was* the Theosophical Society. Her *Secret Doctrine* is the important nucleus of the Theosophical Society. Mathers' writing for the Order is the nucleus of the Golden Dawn. Neither of the two Societies could have existed without these fantastic personalities.

Mr. King evades all of this—and I write this without criticism or rancor—by the assumption (which even he queries) that there was someone in Belgium who was the source of Mathers' materials from which the Order was constructed. In fact, King names a Dr. Thiessen or Thilson of Liege as the Continental Adept, Frater Lux Tenebres, mentioned by Dr. Wm. Wynn Westcott in his 1916 *Data of the History of the Rosicrucians.* This may be true, and I cannot outright deny the possibility of it. But there is evidence of another kind, perhaps not too strong or clear, that German and European sources have to be looked for in tracing the antecedents of the Golden Dawn.

In an appendix to his volume, Mr. King gives the History Lecture as provided by the Order, mentioning that this document was not included in my edition of the Order's lectures and rituals. I ought to state that it was not included simply because I thought and still think that it is an inferior piece of writing which contributes very little factual information. Nonetheless, the opening page of the first chapter of *My Rosicrucian Adventure*

147

consists of three paragraphs extrapolated from that History Lecture.

Incidentally, an example of a practice that I have frequently condemned is provided on page 215 of King's book where the History Lecture supposedly gives the name of the Order in Hebrew—though King is certainly not to blame for this. This Lecture must have been copied so often by students whose Hebrew was defective or nonexistent that what finally appears on that page is meaningless. Mathers originally gave it as *Chabrath Zereh Bokher Aour.*

Earlier in King's volume, there is a minor misunderstanding that Francis King really should correct in later editions. In describing the Qabalistic Cross and the Lesser Ritual of the Pentagram, he states that two of my books, *The Middle Pillar* and *The Art of True Healing,* are little more than amplifications of the Ritual of the Qabalistic Cross and the Pentagram Ritual. Actually, this is most inadequate. *The Middle Pillar* admittedly does give this, but also considerably more. It provides basic instruction in the assumption of God-forms and the Vibration of Divine Names. The source of this instruction was, in the main, the highly informative documents on Telesmatic Images and the Vibration of Names in Volume 4 of *The Golden Dawn,* but also Crowley's Liber O in *The Equinox, Vol. 1, No. 2.* Furthermore, *The Art of True Healing* dilates on and expands a rudimentary schema first outlined in a Portal document in Volume I of *The Golden Dawn.* Fragments have also been drawn from one of the Golden Dawn Z documents which practice had proven to me to be related to the above named rudimentary schema. However, I do agree entirely with Mr. King that the Golden Dawn techniques are capable of almost indefinite expansion. There is much work to be done.

Now we have to consider the second book, that by R.G. Torrens, B.A., and quickly assay all three works in judgmental terms. The first and third books—those by Moore and King—are serious, honest, and good pieces of writting, and the authors need to be highly commended. I cannot make this statement about R.G. Torrens' book which is entitled *The Inner Teaching of the Golden Dawn.*

First of all, several obvious questions arise. Where did Mr. Torrens obtain this inner teaching from? From the Order of the Golden Dawn? Is he a member? We have a right to know. If he was a member, does he realize he has violated his obligations to secrecy? If so, what were his grounds? I personally did violate my obligation to secrecy and I have given a full explanation of my motives for so doing. We cannot expect less from R.G. Torrens. Sometimes, he gives acknowledgement to *The Equinox* of Aleister Crowley and mentions my four volumes of *The Golden Dawn,* but perhaps not often enough!

But before this matter is discussed at some length, the fact must be mentioned that I first learned of R.G. Torrens and his book through an article in a little English magazine *Insight,* issue No. 12, 1969. I have previously had some contact with its editor, Mr. Deric James, with whom I had assumed the existence of a friendly relationship.

In Mr. Torrens' article there are a couple of paragraphs that are just not factual. For example, he states that some former members, amongst others, were Mr. Gerald Yorke, Mary d'Este Sturges, and Ethel Archer. It is not really important, but merely for the sake of the record, it has to be stated that these three people were members of Crowley's A∴A∴ and not the Golden Dawn. It may suggest that our author is not a stickler for accuracy. It may also suggest that our Mr. Torrens has cast too wide a net—and really has missed his fish!

Ethel Archer (Mrs. Wieland) and Mary d'Este Sturges (Soror Virakam) will be found mentioned frequently in *The Equinox,* while the name of Gerald Yorke is known far and wide as the major protector and preserver of Crowley's manuscripts and books. (See, for example, *The Great Beast* by John Symonds.)

The principal paragraph in this *Insight* article which must serve as my target reads as follows:

Crowley's rituals, published in *The Equinox* (Vol. i, No. 2 and No. 3), are incomplete. Regardie's four volume work on *The Golden Dawn* was probably based on the documents stolen by Crowley from the headquarters and are therefore suspect. It varies somewhat from the originals, but read in conjunction with Crowley's work, it does give a fairly reasonable account of the whole.

After having read this article and finding it altogether inaccurate, indicating that Mr. Torrens probably was not too familiar either with *The Equinox* or my own work, I wrote a letter to the editor of the magazine. I hoped he would either forward it to Mr. Torrens or publish it under the caption of "Readers Letters." To date there has been only silence. For this reason, the following reproduces the letter sent to the editor of *Insight*:

25 February 1970

Editor,
INSIGHT
Bournemouth, Hants.

Dear Sir,

I have before me your issue No. 12; and am particularly interested in the article "The Golden Dawn" by Mr. R.G. Torrens.

If this gentleman has been doing research into the Order for a number of years, very little evidence of this is noted in the article. For example, he gives as former members of the

Order the names of such people as Gerald Yorke, Ethel Archer, and Mary d'Este Sturges. Surely he is not serious! These were close associates of Aleister Crowley and the A∴A∴.

He also states that when the Revolt occurred the Order split up into several groups, one of them being headed by Dion Fortune. It is a pity that our Mr. Torrens has not read the article by Dion Fortune in *The Occult Review* around 1934 or so. Dion Fortune there narrates that she was expelled from the Order by Mrs. Mathers, then accepted as a member by another branch in Bristol, whose chief gave her permission to form the Fraternity of the Inner Light. At no time did Dion Fortune head a branch of the Golden Dawn.

If these are examples of Mr. Torrens' scholarship, he is damned at the start. When he states that if my book *The Golden Dawn* were read in conjunction with Crowley's *The Equinox* a fair idea of the Order Rituals could be obtained, he demonstrates that he knows nothing of *The Equinox* nor of my book *The Golden Dawn* or *My Rosicrucian Adventure.*

Yours truly,

The trial of the Horos gang did not cause Dion Fortune, as claimed by Mr. Torrens, to dissociate herself from the Order to form a splinter group. This particular scandalous event occurred long before she could even have heard of the Order, perhaps when she was but a child. She came on the scene far later, and her account of what really happened can be read in an article she originally wrote for *The Occult Review* sometime during 1933 or 1934, if I recall aright. It has been reprinted and comprises part of Chapter X of her book *Applied Magic* (Aquarian Press, London 1962).

The Equinox publication of the Golden Dawn initiatory rituals were so severely edited or mauled I should say (perhaps by Capt.

J.F.C. Fuller, though of course with the tacit approval of Aleister Crowley) that it would be altogether impossible to form any coherent idea of what those rituals actually consisted of.

As to Mr. Torrens' claim that my work *The Golden Dawn* was based on documents stolen by Aleister Crowley at the time of the revolt, it would be well to note that Mr. Torrens uses the word "probably", thus saving himself from having to confess that he does not know whereof he speaks.

By the time I had joined Crowley in Paris in October 1928, whatever Golden Dawn manuscripts Crowley may once have had were no longer in his possession, having been lost, stolen, or misplaced. I never saw one of them. How, therefore, my work could have been based on these hypothetical documents I shall never be able to understand.

Moreover, to prove the inaccuracy of Mr. Torrens' assumptions, there are at least two documents which nowhere are mentioned in any of the Crowley writings. One of them is the terminal part of the Tarot documents dealing with the Star Maps relative to the Tarot attributions to the constellations, and the Four Serpent Formulae which Mr. Torrens has quoted at great length. There is simply no evidence, direct or otherwise, that Crowley had even seen such documents; there is not a trace or mention of them anywhere in his published writings with which I am more than moderately familiar, as my *Eye in the Triangle* may indicate.

But there is an even more emphatic assertion of the fact that Mr. Torrens does not know his facts. He has taken the liberty of quoting from my book *The Golden Dawn,* (without acknowledgment) a paper describing the Tarot trumps written by G.H.Soror Q.L. Soror Q.L. is Mrs. Felkin, now passed to her rest. Her paper could not have been written when Crowley was a member of the Order up to the year 1900. In fact, I doubt if it could have been written until well after 1910. If my book were based on Crowley's stolen documents, how could I have copied something Crowley had never owned or even seen? And beyond this, there is now the fact that Mr. Torrens has quoted this essay from my book without acknowledgment or he has quoted it

152

directly from Order documents he has received, in which case he has violated his solemn obligations to secrecy. And Mr. Torrens wishes to accuse me of having copied from Crowley's stolen documents?

When originally *My Rosicrucian Adventure* was written, the statement was made that I had no compunction, under the circumstances, of publishing the Order's teachings in order to preserve them for posterity, but would not reveal the names of the Chiefs of the Temple (or its members) to which I had once belonged. Mr. King apparently knows something of this, for in a correspondence with me he has guessed to which Temple I had belonged. Not so our Mr. Torrens. I would not like to retract my former statement, but if Mr. Torrens would record of what Temple he is a member, and give the names of his Chiefs, I will gladly write an editorial letter to another English magazine *Pentagram* giving the names of the Chiefs of my former Temple and its location. If Mr. Torrens will not do this, then he owes me an apology, not in private, but in public. I am sure the editor of *Pentagram,* Mr. Gerard Noel, will be happy to publish it.

I am truly sorry that I cannot reproduce here for the sake of Mr. Torrens a copy of my Order examination book. It carries within it the signatures of G.H. Sorores L.O.E. and Spes, and Frater Labore et Concilio. However, this was stolen along with most of my Golden Dawn regalia and paraphernalia when my house was broken into and robbed in February 1969.

The editing of the initiatory rituals of the Order (it makes no difference if we call it the Golden Dawn or the Stella Matutina or the Alpha et Omega, as Mr. Francis King has indicated) was *not* done by me. This information is solely for the benefit of Mr. Torrens. But whoever did do it, managed to do a fairly intelligent job of revision. Nothing of value was really eliminated, Mr. Torrens notwithstanding. Originally the Hierophant, when opening the Temple, would conduct a round of questioning each of the several officers as to his duties, functions and symbolism. These redundant questions were finally eliminated as being entirely too pedestrian, prosaic and time-consuming. Instead, each officer, without prompting, recited his own appropriate lines, simply and without compulsion. This is the *major* (not the only) revision of the older Golden Dawn rituals as performed within the Stella Matutina.

There are two or three other matters to be mentioned, and then the matter can be laid permanently to rest. On page 142 of his book, and then again on page 157, Torrens mentions that the 12th Path on the Tree of Life is The Juggler or Magician, attributed to the Hebrew letter *Bes*. The Golden Dawn manuscripts and most contemporary books on the Qabalah (which Mr. Torrens repeatedly writes as Quabalah, regardless of whether he is quoting Crowley, Dion Fortune or myself) give the second letter of the Hebrew alphabet as *Beth*. This is the customary Sephardic or Israeli pronunciation. Nowhere else save in my earliest book *A Garden of Pomegranates* is it given as *Bes*, which is simply the Ashkenazi variant of that letter, as explained in that book and in one note in Vol. 1 of *The Golden Dawn*. Do you think our Mr. Torrens has had the courtesy of acknowledging the fact that he is quoting from me?

Furthermore, in giving some very strange references to the study of the Tarot, he leaves out one of the most important of *all* recent writers on that subject—Paul F. Case. The latter was once a member of the Golden Dawn in the United States, and though there are a few variants from orthodox Golden Dawn dogma, as it were, he still remains the most prolific, authoritative, and significant of all modern contributors to this field. Mr. Torrens even has the affrontery to quote in his bibliography McGregor Mathers' little book on the Tarot, which is one of the most worthless things ever written, no doubt to obscure the possibility of the uninitiated ever guessing that he knew the correct attributions.

Finally, Mr. Torrens seems to have delusions that the Crowley pack of Tarot cards so exquisitely painted by Lady Frieda Harris bears some resemblance to the Golden Dawn pack. It almost appears as if he had never seen the Golden Dawn pack of Tarot cards. The latter is described at great length in Vol. VIII of *The Equinox* and in Vol. 4 of *The Golden Dawn*. Crowley's trump cards fully described in his *Book of Thoth*, based on his own meditations and spiritual research, bear absolutely no relation to the former.

My own set of the Golden Dawn Tarot cards were stolen when my house was broken into, as already stated. Fortunately, however, a long time ago I lent them to a woman friend in New York, a co-Mason and now the head of an occult order of her own, who had them photostated. From her, I have just obtained a copy of the photostat sheets, each listing about a dozen or twenty of the cards. One of these days, when leisure permits, I propose working with an artist to reproduce a full set of these Golden Dawn Tarot cards for publication. If and when that task is completed, I shall be happy to send Mr. Torrens a complimentary pack of these cards, simply to let him know that he is far from knowing the facts.

Apart from these comments—though it has nothing to do with the history of the Golden Dawn—I must register the opinion that, apart from quoting Crowley and my *The Golden Dawn* without acknowledgment, Mr. Torrens has used more padding in his book than any other I have seen in a long time. About the only worthwhile comment possible about this otherwise ridiculous book is that it fulfills some of my own comments in the Introduction to the new edition of *The Golden Dawn* (Llewellyn Publications, St. Paul, 1969). There I had noted that there was such a mass of new practical material in *The Golden Dawn* that some students complained that they felt overwhelmed and burdened by it. Recommendations were made as to how to handle this phenomenon. If the redundant material or padding in Mr. Torrens' book were eliminated, his simplification *might* serve as fair introduction to the practical magical work of the Order.

Now that that this work of criticism is over, there is little else to say. The history of the Golden Dawn after it was established in England is now fairly well known. If we take this book *My Rosicrucian Adventure, The Unicorn* by Virginia Moore, *Secret Rites of Occult Magic* by Francis King, and *The Eye in the Triangle* which is my attempt to reinterpret Aleister Crowley's history, the facts become pretty clear. In passing, I ought to mention that Crowley's reputation as a black magician was, in large measure, first promulgated by early members of the Golden Dawn who resented his activity on behalf of McGregor Mathers during the revolt. Francis King's book very beautifully demonstrates the meaning of the aphorism about "the pot calling the kettle black." It appears that it was those early members who actually attempted black magical attacks on Crowley himself.

All we *need* now are two additional items. First and foremost, a biography of McGregor Mathers, which has to be written by one of the younger men on the occult scene today. Further an investigation is required into the historical antecedents of the Golden Dawn on the European continent. I am given to understand that something of this kind is being attempted now by another English writer. I await this latter piece of work, not with bated breath, but with considerable anticipation.

No—my work clearly is not done, as once I thought it was. New avenues are constantly being opened up, and as they are explored and investigated, further reports must be made to that portion of the occult public interested in such matters.

Once more then I close this Postscript with the ancient salute. *Vale Fratres et Sorores. Roseae Rubeae et Aureae Cruceae. Benedictus Dominus Deus noster qui dedit nobis hoc signum.*

Sub umbra alarum tuarum, Yod he vau he.

Israel Regardie

Studio City, California
December 1, 1970

CHAPTER SEVEN

SUSTER'S ANSWER TO HOWE

MODERN SCHOLARSHIP AND THE ORIGINS OF
THE GOLDEN DAWN
by
Gerald Suster

It has been said that most occultists are distinguished by their extraordinary ability to believe a dozen impossible and contradictory things before breakfast. This does much to explain the unfortunate fact that the standards of scholarship in the fields of Magic and the Occult are for the most part, so lamentably low. For example, the pretentious, turgid and frequently meaningless bombast of A.E. Waite was for decades termed 'scholarly' by many occult students, a laughable idea to anyone acquainted with the most elementary notions of academic discipline. It is therefore refreshing to encounter a book on the origins of the Golden Dawn Order which has won praise [sic!] in reputable quarters for its standards of scholarship. I refer to *The Magicians Of The Golden Dawn: A Documentary History of a Magical Order 1887-1923*[1] by Ellic Howe.

Ithell Colquhoun, author of the extremely stimulating *Sword of Wisdom: MacGregor Mathers and 'The Golden Dawn*[2] considers Howe's book to be 'the most scholarly' study of the subject. Francis King, himself the author of a very good book on the Golden Dawn and its offshoots, *Ritual Magic in England, 1887 to the Present Day*[3], states that Howe's work is 'brilliantly researched' in his *The Magical World of Aleister Crowley.*[4] demanding our most acute scrutiny and profound consideration, for it purports to prove conclusively that the Order of the Golden Dawn was founded on a number of frauds, and there are many intelligent readers who accept Howe's proof as conclusive.

Mr. Howe disclaims any involvement with occultism and presents himself as an historian of ideas. Students of the occult will perhaps be relieved to learn that Mr. Howe's academic credentials are less than intimidating. So far as I am aware, he holds no position at any recognised University. I am reliably informed that in his youth, he passed some time at Oxford, but that institution did not see fit to reward his studies with a degree, and nor has any other. Academically, then, he is an amateur of history, like the present writer, though it is clear that he has laboured long and diligently to impart University standards to his work. Unfortunately, he has not always succeeded. His first book, which was published as *Urania's Children* in England and as *Astrology: A Recent History Including the Untold Story of its Role in World War II* in America, has the following extraordinary statement in a footnote on page 73: 'Modern Cabalist works by such occultists as Dion Fortune *The Mystical Qabalah* and Israel Regardie, *The Tree of Life,* 1932, can be safely ignored.' Most authorities on the subject would be astonished by this baffling display of ignorance: one can only conclude that Mr. Howe's statements on Qabalah should also be safely ignored. One hopes that Mr. Howe will not disgrace himself further in his second book on the Golden Dawn, though, in Bertrand Russell's phrase, we don't trust a man who drops eggs with H-bombs.

And Mr. Howe's book is in the nature of an H-bomb for those who believe that the Golden Dawn had a more than prosaic origin. This position will now be summarised briefly. In 1887, a set of cypher manuscripts came into the hands of Dr. William Wynn Westcott, a London coroner interested in occultism and Freemasonry. The code, a simple alphabetic one of sixteenth century origin, was soon deciphered by Westcott, revealing a skeletonic description of five hitherto unknown rituals of a mystical nature, and the name and address of one Fraulein Sprengel, who lived in Germany and was allegedly a high-grade Rosicrucian initiate. Westcott asked an occult scholar, S. L. Mathers, to assist him: Mathers agreed to write a series of suitable rituals based upon the skeletons. Westcott wrote to Fraulein Sprengel, receiving in return permission to found an Order and so the Golden Dawn began. In 1891, a letter apparently came from Nuremberg informing the English chiefs that Fraulein Sprengel had died, that the German Lodge was breaking off all correspondence and that enough knowledge had been given out for the Golden Dawn to formulate its own links with the Secret Chiefs.

160

These Chiefs were alleged to be similar to the hidden Masters of Madame Blavatsky's Theosophical Society. In 1892, Mathers claimed to have formulated a link with them, and supplied rituals and teaching for the Inner Order, The Red Rose and the Cross of Gold, which became the controlling force behind the Golden Dawn. Around 1897, Westcott gave up his authority in the Order he had played the major part in founding, leaving Mathers in control. A series of personality clashes provoked many members to revolt, and in 1900, the Order began to fragment into a number of factions which sometimes indulged in undignified squabbling. Legitimate and illegitimate descendants of these factions have nevertheless survived to this day.

Mr. Howe is of the opinion that this account of German Rosicrucian origins and Secret Chiefs is irrational nonsense, and his opinion cannot be lightly dismissed. One can only congratulate him on his patience and industry in the discovery of sources and one must applaud the painstaking nature of his researches. No other writer on the matter has had access to as many relevant historical documents and Mr. Howe has certainly made a most interesting contribution to the Golden Dawn studies. Furthermore, he has brought to his labours a background in the printing industry, and during the war, he specialised in 'document manufacture' and so, as he puts it, '(I) am therefore not without experience in assessing papers.'

There are certain defects in Mr. Howe's book. His history lacks the wit of Francis King, though there is displayed throughout a most laudable investigative tenacity. The style is very dry, with the result that it is sometimes dull. Serious students may perhaps be puzzled by Mr. Howe's occasional tendency to indulge his own facile humour at the expense of the Golden Dawn membership and there is a veiled hostility to the Order's aims which may perplex those accustomed to objectivity in matters of scholarship. Indeed, it may well be asked why Mr. Howe should write two books about matters for which he has scant respect, though that is surely a problem for Mr. Howe to solve. Those who believe that an open mind is the first condition of apprehending truth, will be surprised by Mr. Howe's failure to explain why so many intelligent and talented people of that period chose to join the Golden Dawn and participate in its training. That is the principal deficiency of this author's otherwise earnest work. In short, he may be Ellic Howe but he is not Ellic Why.

Nevertheless, the research of Mr. Howe and the arguments based upon it [sic!] do deserve to be treated with respect. It is time that his position was set forth and considered. His arguments are as follows:

1. Fraulein Sprengel did not exist.

Mr. Howe went to Germany and tried to discover traces of a Golden Dawn type Order during the period 1860-90, but he found no evidence of one. Nor was he the first to investigate the matter. Dr. Felkin, at one time the chief of a Golden Dawn descendant, the Stella Matutina, later made frantic efforts to find Fraulein Sprengel or anyone connected with her during the 1906-1914 period, as did Gustav Meyrink, author of *Der Golem*, during the 1920's. Neither succeeded.

2. The letters between Sprengel and Westcott are crude forgeries.

Mr. Howe laid these letters before Herr Oskar Schlag of Zurich, an eminent graphological specialist. In Herr Schlag's opinion, no one born and educated in Germany would have committed the orthographical and grammatical errors in these allegedly German letters, which also contain frequent anglicisms.

3. Westcott faked documents and correspondence in order to found an occult Order.

According to Mr. Howe, Westcott wanted to attract members by claiming an ancient origin for the Order. He therefore invented a Rosicrucian woman who could not be traced, and who conveniently died as soon as the Golden Dawn got going.

4. Mathers was aware of the forgery.

On February 16, 1900, Mathers wrote the following to Florence Farr, Chief of the London Temple: 'He (Westcott) has NEVER been *at any time* either in personal or in written communication with the Secret Chiefs of the Order, he having *either himself forged or procured to be forged* the professed correspondence between him and them, and my tongue having been tied all these years by a previous Oath of Secrecy to him, demanded by him, from me, before showing me what he had either done or caused to be done or both.'

5. Westcott failed to refute the charge.

On 20 March 1900 (probably), Westcott wrote to W.B. Yeats and investigative committee which had been set up, saying that *legally,* could not prove the details of the origin and history of the Golden wn. 'How can I say *anything* now?' he asked, and he declined to ment on Mathers' accusation. Forgery is a serious accusation, I one would expect anyone accused of it to be indignant. But no. stcott neither affirmed nor denied the charge.

Westcott was alleged to be psychologically unstable.

Mr. Howe showed various samples of Westcott's handwriting to an erienced British graphologist, Mr. Francis Hilliger. At first, Mr. liger would not accept that these samples had been written by the e person. Finally, he concluded that Westcott was an interesting e of multiple personality.

The cypher manuscripts show no evidence of a Germanic origin. he code, as previously stated, was of sixteenth century origin and available in the British Museum.

Mathers never encountered the Secret Chiefs.

n 1916, Westcott alleged that the materials on which Mathers ed his Second Order rituals and teaching were derived, not from Secret Chiefs, but from a Continental Adept, Frater Lux e ebris. Various Golden Dawn members claimed that this gentleman Dr. Thiessen or Thilson of Liege. Mr. Howe has been unable to tify him, although Francis King wrote that he had been 'fairly ably informed'[5], that the name of Dr. Thilson was well known in gian Martinist circles at around the turn of the century.

Secret Chiefs do not exist.

Mr. Howe does not state this proposition openly, but it is clear he umes that these beings are taken seriously only by fools, the chologically disturbed and occultists.

here are also a number of writers who have put forward uments which support those of Mr. Howe.

. Gerald Yorke.

former disciple of Aleister Crowley, Mr. Yorke has written the eword to Mr. Howe's book and endorses his position.

. A. E. Waite.

lthough Mr. Waite is not to be regarded as an authority on

anything other than the language of pomposity, his conclusions
the matter are not devoid of interest. In his autobiography, *Shado*
of Life and Thought,[6] he expressed his views that the original Cyph
Manuscripts were produced between 1870 and 1880; that they we
not the work of Westcott or Mathers; 'that it is unsafe to challen
their remote German connections. . .'; but that 'a pretended Warra
which was exhibited to Neophytes was no better than a sole
mockery'; 'that the Rite laid claim, by implication or otherwise,
remote antiquity; and that it was to this extent a mounteba
concern.'

12. Arthur Machen.

This gifted and sadly neglected author was a member of the Gold
Dawn in the period 1899-1901. In his *Autobiography*[7], he claim
that it shed 'no ray of light upon my path', and derided the Order
founded on a fraud for two reasons: Firstly, the Cypher Manuscri
were written on paper that bore the watermark of 1809 in ink that h
a faded appearance. 'But it contained information that could
possibly have been known to any living being in the year 1809, t
was not known to any living being till twenty years later.' Fran
King concurs: '. . . the actual rituals used. . . because of the knowle
of Egyptian archaeology displayed in them, cannot be dated bef
the second half of the nineteenth century.'

Secondly, Machen argued that ancient rituals are founded on
mythos and on one *mythos* only. But the Golden Dawn 'embraced
mythologies and all mysteries of all races and ages, and *referrea*
attributed them to each other and proved that they all came to m
the same thing; and that was enough! That was not the ancient fra
of mind; it was not even in the 1809 frame of mind. But it was v
much the eighteen-eighty and later frame of mind.'

13. Louis T. Culling.

In his *A Manual of Sex Magick*[8] the late Mr. Culling argued t
Dr. Westcott 'certainly was not the kind of man to be an active pa
in perpetuating a hoax', but then went on unwittingly to demonst
that probably he was. For in Paris 1894, a Mr. Clarke Wal
purchased a United States Charter of something called The Pallad
Order for the suspiciously large sum of $2000. This charter

roduced on page 89 of Culling's book, and bears the signatures of
: Order's chiefs: Diana Vaughn, Dr. Battaille, Leo Taxil and Dr. W.
estcott.

Now, the Palladian Order has been expertly studied by H.T.F.
odes in *The Satanic Mass*[9] and by Christopher McIntosh in
iphas Levi and the French Occult Revival[10], and there is no doubt
atsoever that it was a hoax at the expense of the Catholic Church,
rpetrated by a fascinating practical joker called Gabriel Jogand.
is man made a good living from writing ostensibly anti-satanist
ces under the name of Leo Taxil. Diana Vaughn was his creation.
. Bataille was the pseudonym of one Charles Hacks, author of
other sensational work on satanism.

On April 19, 1897, Jogand announced publicly and gleefully that he
d invented the Palladian Order in an endeavour to ridicule the
urch he despised. It is clear, therefore, that Westcott *was* party to a
ax, though we do not know how actively he participated.

Given this devastating bombardment of rational argument, supplied
h the plentiful ammunition of thorough research, one can hardly
me students of the Golden Dawn for concluding that the gold is
sel and the dawn is false.

t would be unwise, however, to let the matter rest there, for there
a number of questions which need to be asked and considered if we
to arrive at the truth of the matter.

Where did the Cypher Manuscripts come from?

n *Ritual Magic In England,* Francis King argues that when Fred
ckley, 'the mystic', clairvoyant and would-be magician died in
5, some of his papers passed into the hands of the Reverend
.A. Woodford, a gentleman much interested in Masonry. Woodford
covered the Cypher Manuscripts among these papers, and sent
m to Westcott. Ellic Howe points out that the evidence for this
tention consists of a memorandum in Westcott's handwriting of a
versation with Woodford, February 1886, and a letter, again in
stcott's handwriting, which purports to be a copy of a Woodford
sive, and is dated 8 August 1887. This letter states, regarding the
her Manuscripts: 'It confers upon the possessor who understands
meaning to grant the old Rosicrucian secrets and the grades of the

. . . Golden Dawn. Try to see old Soror 'Sapiens Dominabitur Astri
in Germany. She did live at Ulm. Hockley now being dead I know
no one else who could help you.'

This is of interest because Soror S.D.A. was allegedly the magic
motto of the elusive Fraulein Sprengel, and this motto is used on
number of documents, including the Warrant granting authority
the Golden Dawn chiefs. Woodford implies that he had never seen t
sheet which identified her with Fraulein Sprengel and gave
accomodation address in Stuttgart: but the explanation for that
obvious. That information is in code, and it was not Woodford b
Westcott who deciphered the manuscripts.

Mr. Howe is on rather stronger ground, however, when he not
that there is nothing available in Woodford's own handwriting, a
so Westcott may have forged the Woodford letter and fabricated t
conversation with him in which the existence of the Cypher MS. w
first revealed.

Is this really likely? No one, not even Mr. Howe, has accused the
It is virtually impossible to tell. One story has Woodford finding t
manuscripts in a bookstall on the Farrington Road. Or we can belie
Francis King's suggestion that they came from Hockley. But if s
where did Hockley get them from?

According to Francis King: 'the grades. . . of the Golden Dawn we
based on those of the Masonic Golden Rosicrucians of the eighteen
century.' However, the nature of the skeletonic rituals makes o
inclined to accept the view of Francis King, Arthur Machen and A.
Waite that the Cypher Manuscripts were composed between 1860 a
1880 -- by whom and for what purpose? Waite suggested that th
may have been '(a) the inventor's first draft of a projected Rite or (
the jottings of a Member made for his private use, being summa
notes of ceremonies witnessed by himself.' If the latter, whe
Comments Mr. Howe: 'this mystery may never be solved.'

Arthur Machen was for once unjust in claiming that the manuscri
are fraudulent in nature because the paper bore the watermark
1809. This in itself means nothing. It is not unusual for paper of go
quality to be kept for decades and used only for certain special tas
For example, Israel Regardie still has blank paper given to him

eister Crowley which the latter purchased around 1910 on which to
int the *Holy Books*.

Nor is the fact that the cypher can be found at the British Museum
cessarily fatal to the claim that the Golden Dawn had its origins in
rmany. Supposing that Fraulein Sprengel existed, she could well
ve had access to the *Polygraphiae* of the Abbott Johann Trithemius
62-1515): the cypher alphabet and its key is in the Paris edition of
61.

One could construct an interesting hypothesis by following up Mr.
ancis King's opinion that the Cypher MS. were owned by Fred
ockley, who collected magical texts, and who had been a pupil of
ancis Barrett. Barrett's *The Magus* (1801) played a significant part
the English magical revival in the early nineteenth century.
oreover, Hockley's own pupil, Kenneth R.H. Mackenzie 'claimed
it he had been initiated into a continental Rosicrucian fraternity by
Austrian named Count Apponyi. It is interesting to note that
meone of this name was attached to the Austrian Embassy at a time
en it is known that MacKenzie was also there.[12]' Then did the
pher MS. indeed have a Continental origin? 'It does not appear
cessary to take MacKenzie's alleged Rosicrucian affiliations very
iously,' writes Ellic Howe; 'in any event no contemporary German
sicrucian group can be identified.'

This is not quite the case. On page 134 of Gershom Scholem's book
om *Berlin to Jerusalem*, there is mention of a so-called Frankfurt
wish Masonic Lodge, named Chabrath Zereh Boqer Aour [translated
o English as The Hermetic Order of the Golden Dawn], 'famous in
history of Freemasonry from the days of Napoleon.' Scholem, an
thodox scholar, is usually reliable.

A.E. Waite thought it possible that MacKenzie may have been the
thor of the Cypher MS. Although Mr. Howe treats Waite with the
dain he deserves, there is something to be said for the latter's
gestion, which has been endorsed by Francis King and Isabel
therland in *The Rebirth of Magic*. '(Mackenzie) spent a good deal
ime in Europe -- both his German and French were excellent -- and
at least possible that working notes made by him of rituals he had
nessed in some continental magical temple supplemented by

167

extracts from the writings of Levi and bits of Enochian magic were ♦ basis of the occult cipher manuscripts. . .'

The Cypher MS. include information on the corresponden♦ between the twenty-two Paths of the Qabalistic Tree of Life and ♦ twenty-two Greater Trumps of the Tarot pack. The earliest kno source of this was Eliphas Levi's *Dogme et rituel de la haute Ma* (1856). MacKenzie visited Levi in Paris in 1861.

Furthermore, as Mr. Howe has discovered, MacKenzie's ♦ *Royal Masonic Cyclopaedia* (1877) contains a table of Rosicruc: grades, including the phrase 'Pereclinus de Faustis', which was use♦ the Golden Dawn Zelator ritual.

However, we cannot be certain. If the whole business was ♦ sufficiently complicated already, Francis King states that much♦ MacKenzie's book was in fact compiled by our old friend, Reverend Woodford. Moreover, according to Westcott's 1886 men randum of his conversation with Woodford: 'he had once sho♦ K.R.H. Mackenzie a sheet of them (the Cypher MS) and K.R.H. ℕ expressed ignorance of it and wonder. . . The Cypher translates i♦ English, yet they came to (him) from a correspondent in France wi♦ history that they had passed through Levi's hands....'

A German Rosicrucian Order? Eliphas Levi? Kenneth MacKen. Fred Hockley? Another member of the Rosicrucian Society England? Mr. Howe might object that all this is pure speculation which documents cannot be produced. Nevertheless, any of th♦ suggestions may be true. As Professor A.J.P. Taylor observes in essay *The Rise And Fall of Diplomatic History*[13], document history has failed to enlighten us much about the causes of the F World War and most other topics, and its achievements have b♦ disappointing.

However, we can only conclude that the Cypher MS were autho♦ between 1860 and 1880, most likely in the 1870's, and that t♦ authorship and origins remain a mystery.

2. Who was Soror S.D.A.?

She is first mentioned in Westcott's copy of Woodford's alle♦ letter of 1887. She is then identified with Fraulein Sprengel, who be reached via one Herr J. Enger, Hotel Marquardt, Stuttgart.

we wrote to the Wuerttemberg State Archive at Stuttgart asking the police register to be searched. There was no trace of either Herr ger or Fraulein Sprengel.

here exist the following possiblities: (1) Westcott forged the odford letter and there was no S.D.A. (2) There *was* a Soror .A. known to Woodford and Hockley, but she was not the same son as Fraulein Sprengel and Westcott forged the document which itified the two and gave the address. (3) Soror S.D.A. was the e person as Fraulein Sprengel and *did* exist, although it is quite ossible to establish the fact.

Did Westcott really forge the Sprengel letters?

Ir. Howe's evidence that he did is very strong indeed. Yet we not be totally certain. For what sort of person was he? 'As a oner he was accustomed to sifting evidence with the greatest ible care,' writes Ellic Howe,' -- he is said to have conducted more ten thousand inquests during a period of about thirty years. . .'. reover, Mr. Howe states: 'Judging by his letters, Westcott was a le, friendly man. The ladies in the G.D. were rather fond of their ere Aude', while the male members. . . respected him.' Ithell jhoun has gone further: 'To his students in the GD. . . Westcott t have seemed a darling old pussy-cat of a man -- plump, docile, larly, industrious, addicted to regalia and histrionics. . . if he d avoid saying boo to a goose he would do so. . . I feel that on his , Westcott was hardly capable of the calculated imposture uted to him.' 'I knew Westcott moderately well,' wrote A.E. te, 'and amidst all his follies and pretensions -- I do not believe he was the kind of man who would have forged documents.' Even ster Crowley, who thoroughly enjoyed slinging mud at his fellow icians, could not bring himself to be vicious at Westcott's nse. In an essay written for his *Equinox* magazine, Crowley d: 'I have heard and believe nothing which would lead me to bt his uprightness and integrity.' He then begged Westcott to sit the Cypher MS. with the British Museum, or to state publicly he first obtained them.

iven these testimonies to the character of Westcott, one could try ng forward an alternative hypothesis. He was a sweet, kind and gullible soul who did *not* fake the Sprengel correspondence, anything else. After all, according to Ellic Howe, it is impossible determine who actually wrote the Sprengel letters: the handwriting *not* that of Westcott. His connection with the dubious Pallad Order is easy enough to explain: Jogand fooled him and tricked as easily as he did the Catholic Bishops. Mathers' accusations forgery were prompted by the desire to be the sole autocrat of Order and Westcott did not defend himself because he was frighte of controversy and terrified of Mathers. As Westcott wrote to Y and the investigative committee about these charges: 'If I accep this new story -- Mrs. Woodford (wife of the third Chief who died in 1891) would rightly charge me with slandering her d husband's reputation, for he was answerable for the original hist and if I say (Mathers') new story is wrong I shall be open to vio attack by him and I shall have to suffer his persecution.'

Mr. Howe puts forward Mr. Hillinger's expert opinion Westcott was a fascinating case of multiple personality, and sugg that even though Westcott forged the Sprengel letters, some par him may nevertheless have believed in the existence of the latter. is a perfectly plausible explanation on the face of it, although wishes that Mr. Howe exercised more care in his use of demear psychological labels. For example, he describes Mathers as 'paran Crowley as a 'psychopath', calls his own book 'a mad chronicle' 'intermittent psychopathic qualities' and mentions with approval observation of L. Szondi in *Schicksalsanalyse* (1948) that pati with incipient schizophrenic tendencies are particularly to be identi with occultism, spiritualism, Theosophy and Hinduism. One won what he would think of the gentleman who wrote to the *Satur Review* in December 1932 to express 'the greatest possible inte and approval of *The Tree of Life* by Israel Regardie.' Curio enough, he was a psychiatrist, Dr. E. Graham Howe, and the unc the author under review.

One should also bear in mind that for all his experience, Hilliger is a graphologist, not a psychologist, nor does he seem to encountered a phenomenon like this before. Yet I have in front o two samples of Israel Regardie's handwriting which are as diffe

170

from one another as different could be. The ability to write in strongly contrasted scripts is a curious one, but a psychologist who examined Regardie in 1948 concluded that there was no evidence of psychoneurosis or psychosis. In other words, the diagnosis of Westcott is, to say the least, highly questionable.

Doubt has also been thrown recently on Westcott's connection with the Palladian Order. In *The Rebirth of Magic,* Francis King and Isabel Sutherland state bluntly that Westcott's signature on Louis T. Culling's Palladian Charter was forged. From what we know of the Order's creator, Jogand, this seems likely.

We are left, then, with a problem which is difficult to resolve. Everything we can discover about Westcott leads one to believe that he was not the sort of man who would commit forgery. But on the other hand, there is the analysis of the Sprengel letters by Herr Oskar Schlag. It is most unfortunate that these documents can only be inspected by Mr. Howe and his associates, for a second opinion would be of considerable value. One can choose to accept Mr. Howe's conclusions here, as Francis King has done: or one may say, with Ithell Colqhoun: 'some other explanations may eventually come to light.'

4. Where did the Golden Dawn knowledge come from?

We know that it was Mathers who worked up the skeleton rituals into a workable system, but from where did he get his information? Israel Regardie made some very telling points in an article for *Gnostica News*, January 21 1974. 'If Mathers got the Golden Dawn teachings from books in the British Museum, so insinuates Ellic Howe, I ask for references to such simple matters as the Pentagram Ritual, Skrying in the Spirit Vision, Telesmatic Images, the Assumption of God-forms and many other teachings of the Order. I assure Howe that he won't find them there. I, myself, have spent many months looking for similar origins in the same place amongst the Sloane and Harleian manuscripts.

Nor, on inspection, can Arthur Machen's point that the syncretistic nature of the Order's teachings implies fraud, be allowed. 'There is no doubt that Machen overstated his case,' wrote Francis King and Isabel Sutherland in *The Rebirth of Magic*: 'Similar syncretistic leanings can be discerned in some late classical philosophers, such as Iamblichus, in the Renaissance -- a mosaic of 'Thrice Greatest Hermes' is a feature of one Italian cathedral -- and in the 'occult freemasonry' of eighteenth century France and Germany.'

The situation becomes even more perplexing when we consider the teachings of the second, Inner Order. Mathers claimed consistently that this knowledge was obtained clairvoyantly and also from the Secret Chiefs with whom he had established contact. The resulting system is not only extremely beautiful, but possesses an astonishing complexity and displays a genius for synthesis. In particular, the Golden Dawn recension of the Enochian System, which integrates all the aspects of Order teaching, could have been devised only by a mind of genius. Yet nowhere else in his published works has Mathers displayed the slightest sign of genius. There is intelligence, there is earnest scholarship and little else.

It could be argued that Westcott was right and that Mathers received his teaching from [Frater Lux e Tenebres, Dr. Thiessen, Dr. Thilson], but where did *he* get it from? And it could equally well be argued that Westcott had finally plucked up the courage to slander Mathers in return, for, as Mr. Howe points out, there is no more evidence for the existence of Frater Lux e Tenebres than for that of Fraulein Sprengel.

For the present, this is yet another mystery.

5. Why did Mathers accept the existence of Soror S.D.A.?

Here is another puzzle which no one has managed to solve. Mathers' letter of 16 February 1900, which accused Westcott of forgery seems plain enough. Yet in a letter to W.B. Yeats dated 12 January 1901, Mathers wrote the following about a certain Mrs. Horos: 'I may tell you that on more than one occasion I conversed face to face with the *real* 'Sapiens Dominabitur Astris'' (i.e. Sprengel?) in this woman.' In other words, Mathers believed that the spirit of Soror S.D.A. could manifest in the body of Mrs. Horos, which indicates that he accepted the historical existence of the former. Furthermore, Mathers told Aleister Crowley that Soror S.D.A. had manifested in Mrs. Horos and 'related to him details of a very private conversation he had had with Madame Blavatsky at Denmark Hill.'

172

Mathers subsequently realised that Mrs. Horos was a swindler and worse: the woman was sentenced to seven years penal servitude in 1901 for aiding and abetting her husband in the rape of a young girl. Nevertheless, he continued to believe that Soror S.D.A. had existed, despite his denunciation of Westcott. Why?

Is it possible, as I have already suggested, that Soror S.D.A. *was* an historical personage known to Woodford and Hockley and the *real* S.D.A.? In which case, Westcott *had* falsely identified her with his invention, Fraulein Sprengel? Was this Soror S.D.A. the real source of the Cypher MS? Again, we can be certain of nothing.

6. How valuable a witness is Mr. Gerald Yorke?

Mr. Yorke's Foreword to Mr. Howe's book has done much for the latter's credibility in certain circles. For all students of the occult owe a great debt to Mr. Yorke. He has zealously preserved the papers of his former guru, Aleister Crowley and I can personally vouch for his kindness and willingness to assist enquirers. In spite of this, he ends his essay by saying of Crowley: 'The Golden Dawn had given birth to its first pseudo-Messiah. No more need be said.'

With the greatest respect to Mr. Yorke, a great deal more needs to be said, though this essay is perhaps not the place for it. Here, I might as well mention that the one time I met Mr. Yorke -- and he was extremely helpful -- he told me that 'everything I am today, I owe to Crowley.' Moreover, Mr. Yorke's description of Golden Dawn Temple equipment is taken not from Golden Dawn teaching, but extrapolated practically verbatim from Part II of *Book Four*[14] by Aleister Crowley.

Mr. Yorke was never a member of the Golden Dawn and appears unimpressed by the Order. He states that those inspired by its teachings 'are riding for a fall'. He is of the opinion that the so-called Bornless Ritual results in an inflated ego. Yet this was never used in any official Golden Dawn document. He thinks that the Golden Dawn most certainly was 'founded on a fraud' and also, astonishingly enough that A.E. Waite 'was one of the members of the Inner Order who kept his head' when the latter preferred pontificating about the 'Graces of the Spirit' to doing any honest work: and Waite's obituary on Mathers clearly demonstrates the former's cowardice, pettiness and spite.

In addition, Mr. Yorke makes a number of statements which are incorrect. He is of the opinion that the Obligation in the Neophyte Ritual omits any reference to the purpose to which the powers resulting from the successful practice of magic should be put. However, this is flatly contradicted in *The Complete Golden Dawn System of Magic* (Falcon Press 1983) and thereafter in the paper: 'On the General Guidance and Purification of the Soul'; and in the cautionary address of the Hierophant to the newly inducted Neophyte.[15]

When it comes to the Adeptus Minor Obligation, in which the candidate will 'purify and exalt my spiritual nature so that with Divine Aid I may attain to be more than human and. . . unite myself to my higher and Divine Genius', Mr. Yorke opines that the aspiring magician may imagine that he is God, not a servent of God. Of course he may if he is an egotistical fool, but not if he has read 'On The Microcosm' in *The Complete Golden Dawn System of Magic*, where it is stated that the higher Genius is but an Angel on one of the lowest hierarchical rungs, as it were, of a vast spiritual ladder, beyond which are mighty archangelic and divine forces, a proposition which should be enough to humble anyone.[16]

Mr. Yorke's reputation has been honestly earned, but his Foreword adds little lustre to it.

7. Is it possible that there are Secret Chiefs?

Madame Blavatsky clearly thought so; so did Mathers; so did Crowley; so have many who have taken up the practice of Magic. However, it must be said that this search for Secret Chiefs, in which so many Golden Dawn members indulged, seems to be devoid of the slightest profit. If there are such beings, they cannot be discovered, and some would argue that you know about them only when they come and find you.

But can one take this sort of thing at all seriously? J.W. Brodie Innes, novelist and Chief of a Scottish branch of the Golden Dawn, held that it did not matter whether the Gods or the Secret Chiefs actually exist. The point is that the Universe behaves as though they do.

If this seems absurd, one should remember that the notion of the

Earth being round was considered similarly so during the Middle Ages.

I am not competent to pronounce on the matter. I can only recommend that anyone interested in the question should take up Magic and see what happens.

8. Does this issue of origins really matter?

Obviously it matters to anyone interested in the history of ideas. In another sense, though, it does not. For example, let us suppose that a Mr. Smith heads a society dedicated to the relief of hunger in the world, which society claims ten thousand members and the patronage of Lord Blandford. We investigate Mr. Smith's society and discover that the membership is comprised of forty seven people, that Lord Blandford does not exist and that although Mr. Smith is utterly sincere about relieving hunger, he is also a pretentious ass. Does this mean, therefore, that hunger should not be relieved or that his society is not effective?

It is possible, though no more than possible, that Mr. Howe's conclusions are correct, or at least that some of them are correct. However, I hope I have made the point that matters are much less certain than Mr. Howe so confidently assumes.

9. Does the Golden Dawn system work?

There is a fine summing-up in chapter 24 of *Ritual Magic in England* by Francis King: 'The achievement of Anna Sprengel (if she ever existed), Mathers or his unknown occult teachers, was to synthesise a coherent, logical system of practical occultism out of these scattered remains of a tradition that had been broken up by fifteen hundred years of religious persecution. In the last analysis it is quite unimportant whether the synthesiser was Mathers or someone else: the important thing is that those who have really worked at the system in all its aspects have found that it is effective, that it achieves what it sets out to achieve.' The clarity of Mr. King's judgement does much to recommend his *The Rebirth of Magic*, which has recently been published in England.

This is, of course, the point. It is the point which Mr. Howe ignores entirely and which therefore tempts one to ignore Mr. Howe. Members of the Golden Dawn may have and did display pettiness, gullibility, spite and many other human failings. Some were simply silly, a point which Mr. Howe never tires of making. Yet anyone with the honesty and diligence necessary for working the system discovers that it works for him. Here is something noble and splendid, which requires the fullest exertion of all our faculties and which can enable us to know and fulfil our potential as God's sons and daughters in the glorious Universe we inhabit. Anyone who doubts this should try performing the Lesser Banishing Ritual of the Pentagram daily for six months -- it will occupy less than ten minutes a day -- and record the results. I have done so myself and experienced improvement on every level of my life. Mr. Howe would be well advised to go and do likewise, but it is doubtful if he will for he thinks he knows better.

But what do *we* know as a result of Mr. Howe's endeavours? (1) There is no evidence that Fraulein Sprengel existed, though she may have done, along with Soror S.D.A. who might or might not have been the same person. (2) That it is possible, though by no means certain, that Westcott forged the Sprengel letters or caused them to be forged, no one is allowed to examine these documents except Mr. Howe and his associates. (3) That Mathers' charges of forgery laid against Westcott are therefore possible, though not definitely proven, and that Westcott may have been too amiable and/or too feeble to conduct a defence. (4) That Westcott might or might not have been a case of multiple personality, although this is the opinion of a graphologist, not a psychologist. (5) That it is likely, though not certain, that the Cypher MS. had an English origin: but it is possible they came from France, Germany, or even Austria. (6) That Mathers might have been deluded about the existence of beings called Secret Chiefs, concerning whom we can discover nothing. (7) That the origins of the Golden Dawn are still shrouded in mystery, in common with most magical orders throughout history. (8) That we still cannot determine where the Cypher MS. came from, who Soror S.D.A. was or why Mathers believed in her existence, or where on Earth the Order teachings originated. (9) That the proof of the pudding is in the eating. (10) That Mr. Howe's case should be taken seriously but cannot be regarded as conclusive: the verdict must be that of the Scottish courts when the issue is in doubt: **Not Proven**. (11) That none of this matters that much anyway, not because the Golden Dawn is a trivial matter, but because it is such an important one.

Something, then, has been added to our knowledge by Mr. Howe's worthy and tireless industry, but the results are rather less than impressive. We are still left with enough conjecture to make one applaud Professor Taylor's views on the disappointing nature of documentary history. The Golden Dawn has survived for ninety-five years and one doubts if the life of Mr. Howe's book will be anything like as long. Why? Because the Golden Dawn system can enhance the life of anyone who approaches it with sincerity and Mr. Howe's book cannot. One wonders why he wrote it.

In short, the Golden Dawn has survived and will survive despite all efforts to discredit it because it can enoble its aspirants with truth and beauty, light and liberty, force and fire. Mr. Howe is merely fiddling while the Golden Dawn burns.

Gerald Suster M.A. (Cantab)
Los Angeles, California
1982

NOTES

1. 1972, Routledge & Kegan Paul, London, England. 1978, Samuel Weiser, New York, USA.
2. 1975, Neville Spearman, London.
3. 1972, New English Library, London.
   The same book was published in America as Secret Rites of Modern Occult Magic.
4. 1977, Weidenfeld & Nicolson, London.
5. Ritual Magic In England.
6. 1938, Selwyn & Blount, London.
7. 1923, The Richards Press, London.

8. 1971, Llewellyn Publications, St. Paul, Minnesota, USA.
9. 1968, Jarrolds, London.
10. 1972, Rider & Co., London.
11. Jogand/ Leo Taxil, like Charles Hacks/ Dr. Bataille, pretended to be a devout Roman Catholic who was exposing the satanic character of Freemasonry. His writings claimed the existence of a sinister and world-wide brotherhood of satanists, The Palladian Order, which in fact was his own creation. To add sexual interest to his game, he invented 'Diana Vaughn', a leading satanist of noble birth who was considering conversation to the Church: in fact, she was his secretary. Roman Catholic dignitaries took the writings of Taxil and Bataille seriously because, among other things, they wanted to believe in satanism, and in the satanic character of Freemasonry, and desired to convert the satanic Diana Vaughn. This complex and elaborate practical joke was carried on from 1892-7 and gave Jogand both fun and profit: the $2000 he received from Clarke Walker for the Palladian U.S. Charter might be worth as much as $20,000 today.

One result of Jogand's confession to a large crowd in the lecture hall of the Geographical Society in the Boulevard Saint-Germain was a near riot among the Catholics.
12. King, Ritual Magic In England.
13. Europe: Grandeur and Decline, 1967, Pelican Books, London.
14. 1969 Sangreal Foundation, Dallas Texas, USA.
15. I owe this line of argument entirely to Israel Regardie's review of Howe's book in Gnostica News, Jan. 21, 1974.
16. Ibid
17. 1982, Corgi Books, London.

CHAPTER EIGHT

MATHERS' MANIFESTO

MATHERS' MANIFESTO

Of Greatly Honoured Frater DEO DUCE COMITE FERRO, 7 - 4, Adeptus Exemptus, Chief Adept and ambassador of those Secret and Unknown Magi Who are the concealed Rulers of the Wisdom of the True Rosicrucian Magic of Light unto The Theorici Adepti Minores of the Order R. R. et A. C.

This Manifesto is to be placed in the hands of each Theoricus Adeptus Minor upon his or her attainment of that grade. After he or she has carefully read the same, he or she must send a written statement of voluntary submission in all points regarding the Orders of the G.D. in the Outer, and of the R.R. et A.C. to G.H. Frater Deo Duce Comite Ferro before being permitted to receive any further instruction. Unless he or she is prepared to do this, he or she must either resign from the Order, or elect to remain a Zelator Adeptus Minor only, and he or she hereby undertakes to refrain from stirring up any strife or schism hereon in the Second or First Order.

It is necessary that you, who have now attained the Grade of Theoricus Adeptus Minor after having passed through the numerous examinations on the Secret Knowledge of the Zelator Adeptus Minor grade of the Secret Order, should now understand how that wonderful system of Occult Wisdom has been obtained for you.

Prior to the establishment of the Vault of the Adepti in Brittania (the first Order of the G.D. being there in active working), it was found absolutely and imperatively necessary that there should be some eminent Member especially chosen to act as a link between the Secret Chiefs and the more external forms of the Order. It was requisite that such a member should be one who, while having the necessary and peculiar educational basis of critical and profound occult archaeological knowledge, should at the same time be not only ready but willing to devote himself in every sense to a blind and unreasoning obedience to those Secret Chiefs; to pledge himself for the fidelity of those to whom this wisdom was to be communicated; to be one who would shrink neither from danger physical, astral or spiritual, from privation and hardship, nor from terrrible personal and psychic responsibility; one who, while receiving for transmission the Hidden Wisdom of the Rosy Cross, should be willing to pledge himself under the severest penalties possible that the Order should be worked in conformity with the principles laid down by those Secret Chiefs not only for the present time but in future also; and who should further possess an iron Will unable to be broken by any unlooked for opposition that might arise in the carrying out of those duties; he must further pledge himself to obey in everything the commands of the aforesaid Secret Chiefs 'perinde ac cadaver', body and soul, without question and without argument whether their commands related to magical action in the external world, military action in the external world, or to psychic action in other worlds and planes, whether Angelic, spiritual or demonic, or to the Inner administration of the Order to which so tremendous a knowledge was to be communciated. And that he must further be prepared to abide in any country; to undertake any journey at a moment's notice, or to confront the chances of death, pestilence, or elemental upheaval, if called upon in the course of fulfilling their commands to do so; that he would further undertake, whatever might occur, never to lose faith in the Chiefs of the Order, and to keep his body in such a condition of physical health and especially of vital energy that the ordinary chances of corporeal illness and exhaustion should not be permitted to become any bar to his constant efforts and exertions. All this and yet further conditions were insisted upon as the only pledges under which this Divine Wisdom was to be permitted to be given out; and these had to be confirmed by the most terrible obligations.

I, MacGregor Mathers, S. Rioghail Ma Dhream, 5-6; Deo Duce Comite Ferro, 7 - 4, was the Frater selected for this Work, whom you now know as Chief Adept of the Second Order under the title of Deo Duce Comite Ferro which I had taken upon me.

At my urgent request, my V.H. Soror Vestigia Nulla Retrorsum was allowed to be associated with me in this labour, but only on the condition of pledging herself in the same manner, though to a less degree.

With all this it was insisted upon that I, the aforesaid Frater, and in a less degree the aforesaid Soror, were to be held responsible for any action undertaken through mis-apprehension of the instructions of the Chiefs, no matter in what manner those instructions were to be conveyed.

That yet further, it must not be expected that these pledges should confer upon me any right to expect any abnormal material support or assistance. The conditions in question, being only those on which I was to be allowed so great an honour as to be the Recipient of the Knowledge for transmission to the Order and also that in all this my obedience was not to be passive but the active use of the intelligent and voluntary ministrant of the Magic of the Eternal Gods.

These preliminary conditions having been solemnly undertaken by us, then and then only was I able to proceed to the attainment of the knowledge of the full 5 - 6 Ritual and of the Obligation thereof; and the establishment of the Vault of the Adepts; my quitting England being a necessary preliminary thereto.

The working of the Second Order having been thus initiated I was enabled to proceed to the acquirement of the Wisdom of the Zelator Adeptus Minor Grade for transmission to you. A work, the enormous strain and labour of which it would be impossible for me to exaggerate. For you must not think that the obtaining of this knowledge of the Second Order for you has been merely and simply the somewhat common place labour of translating a heap of unclassified manuscripts ready placed in my hands for that purpose. This might indeed be difficult and fatiguing, but it would be the merest childs' play compared with the herculean task I have been called upon to execute.

Concerning the Secret Chiefs of the Order, to whom I make reference and from whom I have received the Wisdom of the Second Order which I have communicated to you, I can tell you **nothing**. I know not even their earthly names. I know them only by certain secret mottos. I have **but very rarely** seen them in the physical body; and on such rare occasions the rendezvous was made astrally by them. They met me in the flesh at the time and place which had been astrally appointed beforehand. For my part, I believe them to be human and living upon this earth, but possessing terrible superhuman powers. When such rendezvous has been in a much frequented place, there has been nothing in their personal appearance or dress to mark them out as differing in any way from ordinary people except the appearance and sensation of transcendental health and physical vigour (whether they seemed persons in youth or in age) which was their invariable accompaniment. In other words, the physical appearance which the possession of the Elixir of Life has traditionally been supposed to confer.

On the other hand, when the rendezvous has been in a place free from easy access by the Outer World they have usually been in symbolic robes and insignia.

But my physical intercourse with them on these rare occasions has shown me how difficult it is for a mortal, even though advanced in occultism, to support the actual presence of an Adept in the physical body; and such meetings have never been granted to my own personal request but only by their own special appointment, and usually only for some reason of extra vital importance.

I do not mean that in such rare cases of physical converse with them that the effect produced on me was that intense physical exhaustion which follows depletion of magnetism, but, on the contrary, the sensation was that of being in contact with so terrible a force tht I can only compare it to the **continued** effect of that usually experienced momentarily by any person close to whom a flash of lightning passes during a violent storm, coupled with a difficulty in respiration similar to the half strangling effect produced by ether; and if such was the result produced in me, as tested as I have been in practical occult work, I cannot conceive a much less advanced initiate being able to support such a strain even for five minutes without death ensuing.

Almost the whole of the Second Order knowledge has been obtained by me from them in various ways by clairvoyance, by astral projection on their part and on mine, by the Table, by the Ring and the Disc, at times by a direct voice audible to my external ears and that of Vestigia, and at times copied from books brought before me, I know not how, and which disappeared from my vision when the transcription was finished, at times by appointment astrally at a certain place, till then unknown to me, an appointment made in the same manner and kept in the same manner as in the case of those rare occasions when I have met them by appointment in the physical body.

The strain of such labour has been, as you can conceive, enormous. In especial, the obtaining of the Z Ritual, which I thought would have killed me or Vestigia, or both, the nerve prostration after each reception being terrible from the strain of testing the correctness of every passage thus communicated; the nerve prostration alluded to, being at times accompanied by profuse cold perspirations, and by severe loss of blood from the nose, mouth, and occasionally the ears.

You know the extreme and sustained attention and critical judgment requisite to obtain any reliable and truthful answers through the Table or the Ring and Disc. Add to all this ceremonies of Evocation, almost constant strife with opposing demon forces endeavouring to stop the delivery and reception of the wisdom and the necessity of keeping the mind exalted towards the higher Self, while at the same time exercising the critical archaeological knowledge and having to make the many references necessary to detect any misapprehension of meaning of passages in Latin, Greek, Hebrew, Chaldaic, Egyptian, and what not. And you will only then have a faint idea of what my struggles and labour have been. The only one among you who has known the fearful difficulties I have had to contend with has been Sapere Aude, and he has therefore well known that such work could not be done in a hurry and rapidly like mere mechanical transcription, or even like ordinary original composition.

But unless the Chiefs are willing to give me the knowledge I cannot obtain it for you. Neither will I give it to you unless I know that the Order is being worked conformably with their wishes and instructions.

What I discountenance and will check and punish whenever I find it in the Order is the attempt to criticise and interfere with the private life of Members of the Order. Neither will I give the Wisdom of the Gods to those who endeavour to use it as a means of justifying intolerance, intermeddling, and malicious self-conceit. The private life of a person is a matter between himself and herself and his or her God; and no person who has taken the Obligation of 5 - 6, and studied the same can be ignorant of its causes and penalties.

The Temples of the Order are places for the performance of Sacred Ceremonies, and the petty criticisms and uncharitablenesses of social clubs and drawing rooms shall be rigidly banished from them.

To invoke carelessly or inadequately the Divine White Brilliance and the Forms of the Eternal Gods while permitting your mind and lower personality to be filled with uncharitableness towards your neighbour, self-righteous pride, and trivial social considerations, is an abominable blasphemy. It is that taking the Name of God in vain which is a most pernicious sin. For by so doing you cannot touch the God, but instead and in his semblance arouse the evil antithesis.

This I know has been a sin among you during this last twelve months; and be sure that this must bring its reaction; and there is no surer road to this error than the encouragement of the feeling of the Pharisee: 'God, I thank thee that I am not as other men are.' Such a formula, whether expressed or implied, means at once separation from that God who is universal.

Of what use are Second Order centres if they are not places where the Gods and the Angelic Forces are invoked in Spirit and in Truth, and where mystic powers have their abode, and where petty social gossip can find no place.

It is possible for you to be word perfect in all the knowledge of the Zelator Adeptus Minor Grade, and to know all its ceremonies by rote, and yet unless you can really and profoundly grasp their inner meaning, an uninitiated person who has a strong will, faith, reverence, self-sacrifice and perseverance, may be more truly a Magician than you.

Finally the reading of this Manifesto will have made you comprehend the enormous amount of time and energy necessary to obtain the Wisdom of the Second Order. To this must be added the considerable amount of other labour connected with the Order, my own work in the Outer World, and with all this the imperative necessity of keeping my physical health and vital energy always up to full pitch, and at times having had the extra disadvantage of being compelled to earn my own living in the world.

I therefore expect you to aid me in tha work to the best of your ability by carrying out my wishes regarding the management of the Order and by abstaining to the utmost of your power from putting any extra hindrances in my way. I considered it advisbable that you should have both had in your possession and carefully studied the whole knowledge of the Zelator Adeptus Minor Grade before receiving this Manifesto.

S. L. MacGregor Mathers.
S. Rhioghail Ma Dhream.
Deo Duce Comite Ferro.

CHAPTER NINE

YEATS' MANIFESTO

YEATS' MANIFESTO

Is the Order of R.R. & A.C. to remain a Magical Order?
Written in March, 1901, and given to the Adepti of the Order
of R.R. & A.C. in April, 1901.

I.

We are about to make a legal constitution by the vote of all the
Adepti. We must, therefore, go to first principles, and decide
what we mean to do with the Order — whether we intend to keep
it as it has come down to us, or to change it into some new shape.
We have even to decide whether we intend it to remain a Magical
Order at all, in the true sense of the word.

"The majority of the Council" have described themselves as
advocating "a system of carefully organized groups." The
committee which is about to be appointed to draw up laws and
bye-laws will have to consider this proposal or proposals arising
out of it; and as whatever the committee decides upon must come
before you, that it may be legal, you yourselves will have to
decide between system and system. I regret that differences have
arisen among us, but none the less I must submit to you a system
which is not, so far as I can judge from a recent open letter, the
system of "the majority of the Council."

II.

I propose that we neither encourage nor discourage "groups"
officially, while retaining our right to do either in our personal
capacity, but that we endeavour to restore the Order to that state
of discipline, in which many of us found it on our initiation into
the second Order some eight or nine years ago. This can be done:

(1) By insisting on a strict obedience to the laws and by-laws.

(2) By making the giving out of the knowledge lectures
dependent on the passing of examinations.

(3) By giving the highest Degree (or Grade) weight in the
government of the Order, and by retaining the old respect for
the Degrees and seniority.

(4) By restoring the oath taken upon the Cross on Corpus
Christi Day, until recent years, by one of the seniors as a
representative of the Third Order.

The passing from among us of Frater S.R.M.D. has thrown
the whole burden of the unity and continuity of the Order upon
the Order itself. They have no longer the artificial support of
his vigirous and imaginative personality, and must be supported
alone by the laws and by-laws and symbols, by the symbolic

189

personality of the Order, a personality which has, we believe, an extreme antiquity, though it would still be alive and active, had it arisen out of the evocations of these last years. The next few years, perhaps the next few months, will decide whether it has been sufficiently embodied "in London" to bear this sudden burden, and of a certainty if it will bear it, it will do so because we have strengthened and not weakened a discipline that is essentially symbolic and evocative, and because we have strengthened and not weakened a system of Degrees that is a chief element in this magical personality. Everything that can be said against the magical examinations can be said, and has been said, against every kind of examinations, whether of the Civil Service or of the Army or the Universities, while the magical examinations can be defended by an argument that can defend them alone. They are more than a test of efficiency, they are more even than an Ordeal, which selects those who are most devoted to the Order. The passing by their means from one Degree to another is an evocation of the Supreme Life, a treading of a symbolic path, a passage through a symbolic gate, a climbing towards the light which it is the essence of our system to believe, flows continually from the lowest of the invisible Degrees to the highest of the Degrees that are known to us. It matters nothing whether the Degrees above us are in the body or out of the body, for none the less must we tread this path and open this gate, and seek this light, and none the less must we believe the light flows downward continually.

It is indeed of special, perhaps of supreme, moment to give the Degree of Theoricus, the highest Degree known to us, enough of importance to make the Fratres and Sorores look towards it with respect and attention, for the Degree of Theoricus is our link with the invisible Degrees. If the Degree has too little knowledge or too little authority, we must give it knowledge from our intuitions and our intellect and authority from the laws and by-laws of the Order. If we despise it or forget it, we despise and forget the link which unites the Degree of Zelatores, and through that the Degree of the Portal and the four Degrees of the G.D. in the Outer, to the Third Order, to the Supreme Life. When I say increase its knowledge, I do not merely mean increase its erudition, or even its understanding of its traditional knowledge. I think we might readily discover for its Adepti some simple form of meditation to be used at stated periods, some symbolic vigil in the mystic tomb of which ours is but the image, to bind them together in a strong indissoluble bond, and to call among them, and through them into the whole Order, some new descent of the Supreme Life, or may be the presence, whether in the body or out of the body I know not, of some Adept, some great teacher. The link that unites us to that Supreme Life, to those Adepti and teachers, is a double link. It is not merely an ascent, that has for symbols the climbing of the Serpent through the Tree of life and of the Adepti through the Degrees that we know of, but a descent that is symbolised by the Lightning Flash among the sacred leaves, and that should be symbolised, if the Order has not abandoned an essential part of its ritual, by the obligation spoken on the day of Corpus Christi by some senior in the name of the Third Order, which thereby takes upon itself the sins of all the Fratres and Sorores, as wisdom takes upon itself the sins of the world.

The obligation is indeed necessary, for by it the stream of the lightning is awakened in the Order, and the Adepti of the Third Order and of the Higher Degrees of the Second Order summoned to our help.

Because a Magical Order differs from a society for experiment and research in that it is an Actual Being, an organic life holding within itself the highest life of its members now and in past times, to weaken its Degrees is to loosen the structure, to dislimn, to disembody, to dematerialize an Actual Being; and to sever the link between one Degree and another, above all between the Degrees that are in the Heart, in the Tiphereth, in the $5=6$, is to cut this being in two, and to confine the magical life of its visible Adepti to the lower substances of this being. To do this last thing is to create an evil symbol, to make the most evil of all symbols, to awake the energy of an evil sorcery. On the other hand, to create within this Order, within this Actual Being formal "groups," centres of astral activity, which are not the Degrees of this Order, the organs of this Being, is to create centres of life, which are centres of death, to this greater life; astral diseases sapping up, as it were, its vital fluids.

III.

The proposal to substitute for the old discipline, the old tradition, "a carefully organized system of groups," is not only to produce this magical evil, and the complex and obscure practical evils and anomalies which are so obvious that anyone accustomed to the work of societies can foresee them.

These "carefully organized groups" are not to be organized by any committee or Council of the Order, or by any authority recognized by the Order, but apparently by a single member, who will be responsible to nobody. No member, no matter how

191

great his faith in the official teachings of the Order, or in its official government, if he have not perfect faith in this member, will be able to introduce students to the Order lest they come under what he thinks an undesirable secret teaching, at once irresponsible and semi-official.

It may be, indeed, that other members are to be encouraged to form "groups," that the magical teaching of this Order is to pass, as its influence and extent increases, into the hands of a number of Fratres and Sorores, who will hide their perhaps ill-balanced ideas from one another and from the Order as a whole, and thereby escape from that criticism which is the essence of all collective life, and of nearly all sane life, in a kind of rabbit-warren of secret "groups." These "groups" will hide not only their doctrines but their membership from one another, and our Fratres and Sorores will exchange that mutual help and understanding, that fruitful discussion, which a common knowledge and a common practice make possible, for distrust and misunderstanding, or at best for the indifference that must arise among people who life in separate rooms with perpetually locked doors. The Council of the Order will be the first part of the Order to suffer, for a "group," the moment one of its doctrines or one of its more influential members is criticized, can hardly avoid passing from the quiescence of a clique to the activity of a caucus. Sooner or later too, even though these "groups" have but one organizer, they will come to have different personalities, and the Council will become a place of battle between people who vote upon a prearranged plan, uninfluenced by the arguments used in the Council itself. I cannot, indeed, imagine any system so well devised as this "system of carefully organized groups" to bring our Order, or any order or society, to an ignominious end.

Every one of these "groups," if they follow the plan of those already founded, will have a separate numerical arrangement on which it will meditate at stated times, every member representing one of the sephiroth; and will have in its midst what professes to be an Egyptian or other spirit seeking to come into relation with our life. The numerical arrangement and recurrent meditation alone are enough to create a magical personality, having its distinct horoscope, and to call into activity a spirit without any formal evocation; and this personality, if it has any continued life at all, is bound to grow stronger, to grow more individual, and to grow more complex, and to grow at the expense of the life about it, for there is but one life. Incarnate life, just in so far as it is incarnate, is an open or veiled struggle of life

192

against life, of number against number, and of all numbers against unity. The fact that the numerical arrangement, which is the foundation of these personalities, is the same as that of the Order will not identify their interests with that of the Order, any more than the foundation upon the one numerical arrangement of the personalities of men and women, stocks and stones, creatures of air and water, keeps them from warring upon one another and upon the great life they come from. It is but a necessary foundation for their separated lives, for were they not established in the sephiroth they could not exist for a moment. The Powers of Disruption may indeed have discovered that the Order could overcome any attack of a mere Frater or Soror, and have so resolved to create these personalities, that will have each one the strength of many. The more vigorously they evoke the White Light in their recurrent meditation, the more active will their personal life become, the more decisively will it diverge from the general life, the more perfectly will it realize its isolated destiny. The White Light is in itself an undifferentiated energy, and receives its differentiated impulse from the symbol that collects it.

If indeed we must make this change, this transference of influence from Degrees, which are like wheels turning upon a single pivot, to "groups" which will be like wheels turning upon different pivots, like toothed wheels working one against the other, this surrender of ancient unity to anarchic diversity, let us make it as complete as possible. Let us re-shape the Order, Inner and Outer alike, destroying that symbolic Organization which, so long as it exists, must evoke a Being into a continuous strife with these alien bodies within its spiritual substance. For even if it came about at last that every member of the Second Order was a member of some "group," that no one, however despised, stood for the Order only, this Being would be for ever present in dreams and visions, or in that deeper life that is beyond even dreams and visions, seeking to answer the but half-forgotten evocation of the Degrees and symbols, and throwing all into disorder and disquiet. We have no choice but to remain a Magical Order, whose organization is a Talisman, or to become wholly a mere society for experiment and research, with an organization empty of magical significance though sheltering smaller organizations that have a magical significance. If the doctrine of talismans and symbols is true — and if it is not, "groups" and Order are alike folly — there is no position between these extremes that is not dangerous to our spiritual and material welfare.

It must not be supposed that these "groups" will have only such effects in the astral and in the material life as the intellect can foresee, or understand. It is a recognized tradition of Magic that talismans — and every "group" is a talisman reconsecrated at regularly recurring periods — act less often immediately upon the souls of them that use them, than indirectly by an unforeseeable and mysterious action upon the circumstances of life. A group whose astral personality had become active would in all probability bring its separated life to a complete fruition of self-consciousness through circumstances that would arise suddenly and without any apparent relation to itself. It would come to this fruition like a man who, let us say, makes a talisman for courage and grows courageous through being suddenly thrown into some unforeseen danger, which he does not understand has been called up by the talisman. The central principle of all the Magic of power is that everything we formulate in the imagination, if we formulate it strongly enough, realises itself in the circumstances of life, acting either through our own souls, or through the spirits of nature.

IV.

It is said that these "groups" which keep, or try to keep, their doctrines and their membership secret, are necessary for magical progress, that the mere circulation of their formulae among Fratres and Sorores would interrupt Adepti upon their paths. If this idea has been put into the mouths that speak it by beings that seek to grow at the expense of the general life, I understand it; but if it has not, it is unintelligible. Does the circulation of the "Microcosm Ritual" among us make its formulae powerless, or has our Magic been struck by palsy because the Fratres and Sorores of the Outer know our names? It is said, too, that these alien personalities, each one made up of many, are necessary to Adeptship. This argument seems to me sheer dillettanteism, mere trifling! Was Plotinus one of a "group" organized on "the globular sephiroth" when he was thrice united with God while still in the body? It is by sorrow and labour, by love of all living things, and by a heart that humbles itself before the Ancestral Light, and by a mind its power and beauty and quiet flow through without end, that men come to Adeptship, and not by the multiplication of petty formulae. What is this formula of the "groups," the utmost of their present practice as they say, that is to be a ladder into heaven? Now that the secresy is a little faded we know enough of it to know that it is nothing new or wonderful. They use a simple meditation that has for one effect the welding

194

those who use it into one, a little at the expense of their individual souls, which, instead of remaining each a distinct circle, become, as it were, segments of a circle that has no very great or rich life to give them in payment; and for another effect, the awakening of a sympathy, which is limited to those who use this meditation at the same hour and as part of the same sphere. A partly similar meditation is sometimes used by lovers or friends to make their union the closer, to make more intense that love which somebody has called "an egotism of two," and sometimes, and I know one rather terrible case, it makes the union so close that those who use it share not only emotions, but sicknesses and follies. Because of this sharing of all by all, I doubt very much if these meditations should ever be used without certain ceremonial precautions of a rather elaborate kind. In an Order like ours there is, or there should be, the ceremonial sacrifice of one through whom the Third Order takes upon itself and gathers up into its strength, which we believe to be the creation of centuries, the frailties of all. But in a "group" frailty must bear the burdens of frailty, and as it seems without the joy of a conscious sacrifice and with none to lighten the burden but some wandering spirit, itself, it may be, seeking help. Surely Adeptship must come more easily in an order that "reaches up to the throne of God himself, and has among its members angels and archangels," than in a "group" governed by an Egyptian spirit found, it may be, by accident in a statue.

If any were to become great among us, he would do so, not by shutting himself up from us in any "group," but by bringing himself so near to that continual sacrifice, that continual miracle, whose symbol is the obligation taken by the Senior, that he would share alike in its joy and in its sorrow. We receive power from those who are above us by permitting the Lightning of the Supreme to descend through our souls and our bodies. The power is forever seeking the world, and it comes to a soul and consumes its mortality because the soul has arisen into the path of the Lightning, among the sacred leaves. The soul that separates itself from others, that says "I will seek power and knowledge for my own sake, and not for the world's sake," separates itself from that path and becomes dark and empty.

The great Adept may indeed have to hide much of his deepest life, lest he tell it to the careless and the indifferent, but he will sorrow and not rejoice over this silence, for he will be always seeking ways of giving the purest substance of his soul to fill the emptiness of other souls. It will seem to him better that his soul be weakened, that it be kept wandering on the earth even, than that other souls should lack anything of strength and quiet. He will think that he has been sent among them to break down the walls that divide them from one another and from the fountain of their life, and not to build new walls. He will remember, while he is with them, the old magical image of the Pelican feeding its young with its own blood; and when, his sacrifice over, he goes his way to supreme Adeptship, he will go absolutely alone, for men attain to the supreme wisdom in a loneliness that is like the loneliness of death. No "group," no, not even a "group" "very carefully organized," has ever broken through that ancient gate.

V.

If we preserve the unity of the Order, if we make that unity efficient among us, the Order will become a single very powerful talisman, creating in us, and in the world about us, such moods and circumstances as may best serve the magical life, and best awaken the magical wisdom. Its personality will be powerful, active, visible afar, in that all powerful world that casts downward for its shadows, dreams, and visions. The right pupils will be drawn to us from the corners of the world by dreams and visions and by strange accidents; and the Order itself will send out Adepts and teachers, as well as hidden influences that may shape the life of these islands nearer to the magical life.

Those who would break this unity would do so, it seems, if I am to judge by what I read and hear, in the name of freedom. I too might talk of freedom, for I do not recognise as its supporters those who claim the right to do and teach in secret whatever pleases them, but deny me the right to oppose them with the only means I have used or desired to use, criticism; but I have preferred to talk of greater things than freedom. In our day every idler, every trifler, every bungler, cries out for his freedom; but the busy, and weighty minded, and skilful handed, meditate more upon the bonds that they gladly accept, than upon the freedom that has never meant more in their eyes than the right to choose the bonds that have made them faithful servants of law. It was the surrender of freedom that taught Dante Alighieri to say "Thy will is our peace;" and has not every man who ever stooped to lift a stone out of the way, or raised his hand to gather a fruit from the branch, given up his freedom to do something else? We have set before us a certain work that may be of incalculable importance in the change of thought that is coming upon the world. Let us see that we do not leave it undone because the creed of the triflers is being cried into our ears.

D.E.D.I.

In the Mountain of Abiegnos.

196

CHAPTER TEN

ME MODERN ADEPTS OF THE GOLDEN DAWN

Subtle is the Way:
A Personal Portrait of
Dr. Francis Israel Regardie
By Joseph Lisiewski 5-6

ı the recollection of recent history, we have seen much derision
ıe notable characters who were the formulating agents of the
ʏ and Hermetic Order of the Golden Dawn. After the Charter
granted by the German Head, Sapre Aude to the group headed
;. L. McGregor Mathers, the Occult literature of our time has
ıessed incessant attacks against its chief members. Most
bly, the attacks have been leveled against Mathers, Wynn
tcott, Aleister Crowley, and in later times of predecision,
cis Israel Regardie.

is this author's considered opinion, that no accusation can be
ıuately made against anyone, without personal contact with
individual. Indeed, our current presses are filled with
;ations against individuals, based solely on personal biases. In
normal stream of time, any statement will eventually be
pted as true, be it so or not. And this most certainly holds true
re it comes to the character and personality of Dr. Francis
·l Regardie, who was my Mentor and personal friend from the
of our first meeting in 1971 until his death in 1985.

nd so, from this personal, intimate view of Regardie, I would
to recapture that individual, and particularly his unique
ıties. This technique of presentation can only be viewed from
·oint of contact through which I first met him, and extend, as a
ıal evolutionary tract, our subsequent commitment and
ınal work together.

:onsider Regardie's and my first "meeting" Fate (or Chance, if
will). It came about in a most extraordinary way. Even
·wing it now, years later, I still find it holds all of the original
n and fascination which it did in those days, so long ago.

It was New Year's Eve, 1968 when my best friend (now a P
in the Catholic Church) and I conducted an Experiment in Gc
Thurgy: that is, Ceremonial Magic. More precisely within
division, it was an Experiment in Magical Evocation. As
Student of our Art and Science understands, this is a pro
whereby one works from a Grimoire,. or a book of "Mag
Tracts" to evoke a Demon into physical manifestation. Of co
the purpose for this depends upon the Demon evoked, and
particular talents and abilities which happen to lie in direct
with the desires of the Thurgist, or Ceremonial Magician.
Experiment, begun exactly at midnight, proved a complete suc
insofar as the manifestation of the Demon was concerned, but
to certain technicalities, our control was lost, and the Experir
very nearly ended in disaster, to the point of losing our lives, i:
worse!

Over two years then passed. It was now the end of the Sun
of 1971.1 had planned a second Evocation, this time of a
powerful Prince as given in the Goetia (which means literally '
Book of Howling"). And so, the same Assistant and myself en
the Magical Circle, using the Goetia in combination with
Magus. Once again, the Experiment was utterly successful in t
of ultimate manifestation, but in the end, my Assistant and I '
trapped for three days and nights within the Circle, tr
desperately to send It back from whence It came. We fir
succeeded. Completely exhausted, we rested for two entire c
During that time, I came to realize that I was not "suffici
developed" Magically, and sought something which would fil
void. My Assistant returned to the Seminary, and would
nothing else to do with the matter. I was alone.

I was 21 years old at this time, and had an extensive O
library built up: the-highlights included the works of Crov
Mathers, Waite, Regardie, Fortune, Butler, Knight, not to me
old manuscripts and Grimoires. For some reason, I sel
Regardie's book, "The Twelve Steps to Spiritual Enlightenm
as my new Path of progress. I also decided to write to the au
then just another name in my library. But in all gentlem
matters, an introduction is called for. So I wrote a brief letter t
then publisher of the "Twelve Steps," requesting his add
Within six weeks I received a communique from Regardie dir
It read as follows: "Dear Mr. Lisiewski: I am very busy nov

y not have time to get involved in an extensive correspondence.
: do write me, and we will take it from there." And so, I
nposed an extensive letter listing my two Evocations, and
mitted it to him.

lis response was subtle in its wording, but telling and to the
nt. His curiosity was piqued, at least for a letter or two. And so I
)te an extensive letter to him, delineating the course, mani-
ations and subsequent near results of the manifestation of
)cation.

Within two weeks, I had a reply. Regardie's response was again
tle, inquiring about specifics of the Ritual which I provided.
lowing this, we struck-up a relationship: his apparently
idoffish ways, due to his years of dealing with lunatics in the
:ult were overcome. From mid 1971 to mid 1973, we corre-
nded 23 times. Each time, my questions were answered: some
ipletely, some only in part, concluded by a question. It was not
l many years later that I learned the method to his madness: all
vers, given without strain, struggle and development of the
lent are answers without form or substance. I found that he
: enough to direct the Student along the correct Path, but the
lent's individual Spiritual Nature must lead him to the final
tion. In so doing, the Student approaches that enviable goal of
eving the Knowledge and Conversation of the Holy Guardian
el. Our letters dealt with Qabalah, Ceremonial Magic, Skrying
>pirit Vision, Tarot, Geomancy, etc. With each letter, his
iance became more and more apparent to me.

1 September of 1973 we had another long telephone conver-
)n. Regardie felt it was time for us to meet. I was invited to fly
1 my home in Pennsylvania to Los Angeles to meet him. This
the opportunity of a lifetime, and I took it.

ly first meeting with Regardie was most illuminating. He was a
:r small man, but hardly frail in the usual sense. His demeanor
strong and quietly insistent. He had a power of penetration: a
:tration that proceeded from his entire frame, not from merely
:yes, as most people hold to. Still, this forceful power was not
whelming: rather, it possessed a subtle quality. We spent the
two days in concentrated discussion and Ritual. It was during
time that Regardie invited me into the Golden Dawn through
Middle Pillar Ritual, and instructed me in Astrology, and later
e ways of Enochiana. I was now one of his formal Students,

although to the rest of the Occult World, he never admitted taking any formal Students, as he decried in one of his class "The Middle Pillar." Once again, we see one of Francis' sub techniques to keep the leeches of the Occult off his back!

It was not long after our first meeting that Francis introduced to the Head of the A∴A∴ (Argentum Astrum) a Magical Or based on the works of Aleister Crowley, which were actu: derived from the Golden Dawn. I began as Secretary to the Or for two years, and was finally promoted to the post of Chance of the Order, second only to Its Visible Head. This lasted for years, until the Visible Head and I had a severe, public bre which initiated hundreds of letters spread between Regardie, Visible Head and myself. Regardie was delighted!

The rift which finally produced the break-up of the A∴A∴ due to "Alchemical reasons." For it was during this episodic pe with my association with the A∴A∴ Regardie introduced m Frater Albertus (Dr. Albert Richard Riedel) the President and H Lecturer of the Paracelsus Research Society, Utah Institut Parachemistry, Salt Lake City, Utah. It was Frater Albertus brought the hidden aspects of Alchemy into the open, and taug openly in his School of Alchemy. And so, due to Regardie's g graces, I was admitted to that select group of students wh numbered only 12 per year. For seven years I worked under Fr Albertus, and learned everything he had to teach, both theoretic and practically, in the laboratory. Francis was delighted at this he felt that my scientific background in Physics and Enginee could render into a more concrete form the teachings of Alche In no way were the teachings or laboratory practices of Fr Albertus unscientific: quite the contrary. But Francis saw a un opportunity to present things in a slightly simpler manner. was my task. And so it was done. When I introduced it into A∴A∴ I met with the enormous resistance hinted at earlier, only from the Visible Head of the Order but the constituenc well. Everyone insisted on delving into "Spiritual Alchemy" a an important, but secondary form of physical labora manifestation. The rift brought me to leave the A∴A∴, and after that it dissolved.

Once again, Regardie took me under his wing, so to speak, agreed the A∴A∴ had degraded.

Throughout the remaining years, we grew closer and closer. What had started out as a, Mentor-Student relationship now grew into an extremely close friendship. Francis was always ready and available at any time during the day or night to aid me in those problems for which I had no other source to turn to. He displayed the most amazing wisdom in matters which plagued me at the time. His energy was without limits, his compassion without condition, his intelligence without restriction, and his humor and joy of life became a beacon for all those genuine Students of the Golden Dawn to follow.

It is said that the eternal torch must not only burn, but be passed to a new generation, serving not only as a source of Light, but as a source of inspiration. For in the dual aspect of Nature, one cannot exist without the other. And so the torch has been passed.

The memory and force of the Life of Dr. Francis Israel Regardie is immortalized within that flame, as my Mentor, Confidant and Friend. I hope that all of us who lift up the flame will be supportive of Dr. Regardie's wish, that through diversity we each serve the source of the Light.

Joseph C. Lisiewski
Adeptus Minor
Chief Alchemical Consultant of the Hermetic
Temple and Order of the Golden Dawn
February, 1987

Francis Israel Regardie

When a great Magician dies, one is sure to be bored by those who loudly proclaim: "I was his Great Disciple." In Regardie's case, they condemn themselves for he did not have disciples; he had friends. I was proud to be one of them though it was obvious to me that he was older, more accomplished and much wiser than myself.

I first met Regardie in Los Angeles, after a correspondence on Crowley, in the summer of 1971 and found him both impressive and delightful. I especially appreciated his kindness, his modesty ant his gloriously sane and refreshing sense of humour. My return to England meant that I did not see him again until my stay in America 1981-2, which is when we became friends.

At the age of 76, his vim and vigour put many young men to shame. He was a consistently stimulating and charming companion and I treasure the memories of staying at his lovelv home in Sedona. Arizona and enjoying the excellence of his hospitality. He was a man who loved life and this was reflected in the broad range of his interests; he even shared my love of boxing.,He never forced his own views on others — "The divine genius is within you," he used to say "Do it yourself." — though one could always turn to him for sagacious advice.

I had the honour of receiving instruction from him — he was reluctant to teach though superb once he was persuaded to do so — and of witnessing his magical work. Here, his style was calm, authoritative, firm and courteous — yet the power his Magic generated was awesome. There was a pure and shining integrity about, his dedication to the Great Work and this was shown too in his impatience with pretension and inessentials. Whenever he was aked his Grade, he would reply, "I'm a student. We're all students." In my view, Golden Dawn Magic owes its continued survival to the tireless work of Regardie.

He was an excellent writer on Magic and Psychology and performed a lasting service by bringing these two disciplines together. His style was crisp and clear, his contents of permanent value to any seeker after Wisdom. One particularly applauds his technical innovations which gave us the Middle Pillar Ritual and the Opening by Watchtower; and *The Eye in the Triangle,* by far the finest study of Aleister Crowley. *The Complete Golden Dawn System of Magic* is of course his greatest contribution: one might call it the essential compendium of pure Magical Classicism, and all students owe Regardie a lasting debt of gratitude.

One evening when I was sitting with Regardie out on his sundeck and was gazing at the canyons in the distance, I acked him for the greatest piece of wisdom about life that he knew, . "Sounds banal. I know," he replied. "but it's a funny old world." That was in the Summer of 1982 and in the years since then I have found that allegedly banal statement to be Of All Truth on every plane. I can hear Regardie's voice as I am typing this. "Oh, yes," the old man's chuckling, "it's a funny old world."

Gerald Suster
London
February 23, 1987

THE NEW ORDER OF THE GOLDEN DAWN

"Behold! the rituals of the old time
are black. Let the evil ones be cast
away; let the good ones be purged by
the prophet! Then shall this Knowledge
go aright." (Liber Legis, II:5)

Do what thou wilt shall be the whole of the Law.

There is now emerging in the world a New Order of the Golden Dawn. It is a Magical-Religious-Scientific Order dedicated to the vital perpetuation of the teachings of Aleister Crowley and Israel Regardie. The principal function of the New Order is to assist in the initiation of aspirants into the Royal Life of Thelema. It is a Magical Order of the New Aeon wherein men and women, by the essential aids of Science and Religion, can evolve in Freedom, and duly prepare themselves for the Great Initiation into the Illustrious Order of the A∴A∴, that is, the Order of the Silver Star.

The New Order of the Golden Dawn is called in the Latin tongue "Novus Ordo Aurea Aurora". It is further called the Thelemic Order of the Golden Dawn. The Golden Dawn now embraces and upholds the Law of Thelema and seeks to extend that Law in the world, to establish the New Kingdom of Horus upon earth. The Rising God of the New Temple is Horus, the Crowned and Conquering Child, born from the past Aeons of Isis and Osiris. The Old Temple has been transformed into a New Temple for Our Lord Horus to indwell, that the Great Work of the New Aeon may be accomplished in His Name.

The Thelemic Order of the Golden Dawn is operated, supervised and directed by Christopher S. Hyatt, Ph.D. and Sir David Cherubim in association with New Falcon Publications and the Israel Regardie Foundation. Dr. Hyatt was a personal friend and student of the well-known Golden Dawn Magician Israel Regardie,

207

and it was these two men who originally sought to inaugurate the New Order of the Golden Dawn. Since Regardie's death in March of 1985, Dr. Hyatt has been dedicated to the continuation and preservation of this Great Work. Sir David Cherubim, an instructor of Thelemic Magick in the Los Angeles area since March of 1985, was initiated by Dr. Hyatt in the Golden Dawn and has been working with him since then to assist in this vital work, to establish the New Order of the Golden Dawn, and this through the works and teachings of both Israel Regardie and Aleister Crowley.

In October of 1928, Regardie met with Crowley in Paris to become his personal secretary and student; and, unknown to the occult world at large, Regardie was not only initiated by Crowley in his Order of the A∴A∴, but he was also Crowley's Confidential Agent and was initiated by Crowley as a member of the Ninth Degree of the O.T.O. (Ordo Templi Orientis). The current Caliph of the O.T.O., Frater Superior Hymenaeus Beta, has confirmed this fact. (See the documents at the end of this chapter.) In January of 1933, shortly after severing with Crowley as his personal secretary, Regardie joined the Order of the Golden Dawn at Hermes Temple in Bristol, but resigned from this Temple of the Stella Matutina in December of 1934, yet only to become one of the most influential figures of the Golden Dawn Current and Tradition.

Aleister Crowley, like Regardie, was a member of the Golden Dawn. But he joined the Order in November of 1898, shortly before the commencement of its gradual decline in 1900. Crowley was initiated as an Adept of the Golden Dawn in January of 1900, when chaos, not order, became the ruling spirit of its members. At this point in the Order's history it experienced a subtle death, but in April of 1904 Crowley received from his Holy Guardian Angel the Book of the Law (Liber Legis) which proclaimed that he was the Prophet of a New Aeon and that his office was essentially that of being the founder and High Priest of a New Order on earth. This event, I venture to say, was a direct manifestation and result of Crowley's initiation in the Order of the Golden Dawn. The Golden Dawn was, in point of fact, the basis of the proclamation of the New Aeon of Horus and the Law of Thelema.

Without the existence of the Order of the Golden Dawn, the manifestation of the New Aeon of Horus would have made little sense to Crowley and to many another. Thelema would not be what it is today without the existence of the Golden Dawn. And it can be equally asserted that the Golden Dawn would not be what it is today without Aleister Crowley. Crowley rightfully violated his Oath of Secrecy to the Golden Dawn and published all of its Rituals and Teachings in his prodigious periodical called The Equinox. This he did for various reasons, one of which was to preserve the Sacred Tradition of the Golden Dawn. Later Regardie was to do the same in his Complete Golden Dawn System of Magic (New Falcon Publications). Both Crowley and Regardie were Adepts of the Golden Dawn, and not only did they witness its gradual decline, but they also worked toward the preparation of its revitalization and reformation, and it is where they left off in history that we have taken responsibility as rightful successors to their work, to establish the New Order of the Golden Dawn.

Christopher S. Hyatt and Sir David Cherubim have been dedicated to the task of establishing an International Thelemic Society of the New Order of the Golden Dawn since January of 1990. It was in January of 1988, approximately one hundred years after the inception of the Hermetic Order of the Golden Dawn, that these two Magicians first communicated with each other; and when they eventually met in October of 1989, they shortly thereafter determined to unite forces to form and establish the New Thelemic Order of the Golden Dawn. Israel Regardie, in his Introduction to Crowley's *The Law is for All* (New Falcon Publications), predicted that in the beginning of 1990 something momentous was to occur in the course of history, suggesting what Crowley referred to as "a new current…[to] revive the shattered thought of mankind." The fulfillment of this prediction was the inevitable actualization in time and space of one of Regardie's own magical aspirations, to initiate the dynamic current of a New Order of the Golden Dawn; it was also a fulfillment of Crowley's own magical aspiration to promulgate and establish Thelema in the world of men and women.

The Thelemic Order of the Golden Dawn has seven principal grades which compose three groups, the Orders of the S∴S∴, of the R∴C∴, and of the G∴D∴ respectively. These three groups constitute the whole of the Thelemic Order of the Golden Dawn. Before a candidate can progress on the Tree of Initiation, by proper advancement into the following seven grades, he must first endure the trials and tribulations of the probationary grade of a Neophyte (0 Degree). The following is a list of the grades of the Novus Ordo Aurea Aurora in their proper groups.

The Order of the S∴S∴

Ipsissimus .... 7th Degree
Magus .... 6th Degree
Magister Templi .... 5th Degree

The Order of the R∴C∴
(Babe of the Abyss — the link)
Adeptus Exemptus .... 4th Degree
Adeptus Major .... 3rd Degree
Adeptus Minor .... 2nd Degree

The Order of the G∴D∴
(Dominus Liminis — the link)
Zelator .... 1st Degree
Neophyte .... 0 Degree

The seven grades of the New Order of the Golden Dawn are
linked with the seven Chakkras of Yoga, the seven traditional
Planets of Astrology, and the seven Metals of Alchemy. The
system of the New Order is still Qabalistic in structure, but the
method of climbing the Tree of Life is of a slightly different kind.
Moreover, the grade of Zelator is the stage of Birth; the grade of
Adeptus Minor is the stage of Life; the grade of Adeptus Major is
the stage of Death; and the grade of Adeptus Exemptus is the stage
of Life after Death. The other grades of Magister Templi, Magus,
and Ipsissimus pertain to stages beyond man's power to
comprehend; they are spiritual experiences of the most exalted type
and cannot be defined by human philosophic terms. The Third
Order of the Silver Star is beyond man's power to know; he must
experience a different species of consciousness to Understand what
is beyond knowledge, to attain True Wisdom, and to be crowned
with the Celestial Light of the Dawning Aeon of Horus.

The New Thelemic Order of the Golden Dawn is unlike the Old
Hermetic Order in many ways; but the principal difference is that
our Ceremonies and Teachings are dedicated to the essential and
inevitable establishment of the Law of Thelema which is the Law
of the New Aeon. The Hermetic Order of the Golden Dawn, which
was organized in the Old Aeon of Osiris, was subjected to the
awful restrictions and limitations of the past, whereas the Thelemic

210

Order of the Golden Dawn is free from the fetters of the Old Age of Restriction, and its Great Work is the Liberty of every individual in the Dawning Light of the Rising Sun of this New Aeon of Horus. It may be seem a blasphemous or desecrating act to some rigid types that we have dared to combine the energies of Thelema and the Golden Dawn; but as we have only witnessed too well, this essential synthesis of energies has only served to revitalize and perpetuate the Golden Dawn Current, and this in a manner that conforms with the Spirit of the Times; and it has also served to promulgate and establish Thelema in a number of effective and successful ways.

Another important difference between the New and the Old Order is that we work with a sevenfold rather than a tenfold grade system, and this sevenfold system is linked with the Seven Chakkras of Yoga. We also incorporate in our system other elements of Yoga and various elements of Tantra, combining these with various Qabalistic and Alchemical principles, thus uniting both the East and the West. We also work with the Thelemic system of Three Triads set forth in the Book of the Law. Thus the structure of our Order conforms with that of the O.T.O. and other Thelemic Orders, and as such it allows for initiates of these other Orders to enter our Order at their own level or grade without having to undergo grades of a lesser nature. And since there is a link between the grades of the Hermetic and Thelemic Orders of the Golden Dawn, members of the former may enter the latter at their own level without having to undergo grades of a lesser nature. Thus, for instance, an Adeptus Minor of the Hermetic Golden Dawn can be initiated as an Adeptus Minor in our Order without having to undertake the earlier initiatory grades.

Moreover, the New Order adheres to the injunction in the Book of the Law, "...the rituals shall be half known and half concealed." This we freely interpret to denote that the rituals should not be limited to the mere written word, but should be expanded upon to accord with the nature of each initiate. The half that is known is the written words of instruction in a ritual; the half that is concealed is the unwritten personal elements of a ritual. Our rituals are more personalized than the formal and rigid rituals of the Old Order. Of course we have our standard rituals of initiation, but we do not limit ourselves to the written words of these rituals, rather do we expand upon them as each individual case demands. Thus each

211

initiation, though partaking of the same standard ritualisti
elements, are also extemporaneously augmented to accord with th
particular nature and conditions of each initiate. Each initiation i
therefore unique, and not of a mechanical and fixed nature.

Now in the Book of the Law, I: 40, Nuit, Our Lady of the Star:
proclaims, "Who calls us Thelemites will do no wrong, if he loo
but close into the word. For there are therein Three Grades, th
Hermit, and the Lover, and the man of Earth. Do what thou wi
shall be the whole of the Law." The first Grade is the Man of Eart
Triad which concerns the lesser mysteries of the Novus Ord
Aureae Aurora, which is, properly speaking, the First Order of th
degrees of the Neophyte, Zelator and Dominus Liminis; the ne>
Grade is the Lovers Triad which concerns the mysteries of th
Novus Ordo Rosae Rubeae et Aureae Crucis, which is the Secon
Order of the degrees of the Adeptus Minor, Adeptus Major, an
Adeptus Exemptus; and the next Grade is the Hermit Triad whic
concerns the mysteries of the Novus Ordo Argentum Astrun
which is the Third Order of the degrees of the Magister Templ
Magus, and Ipsissimus.

In the Book of the Law, I: 50, Our Lady Nuit further proclaim
"There is a word to say about the Hierophantic task. Behold! the
are three ordeals in one, and it may be given in three ways. Tl
gross must pass through fire; let the fine be tried in intellect, ar
the lofty chosen ones in the highest. Thus ye have star & sta
system & system; let not one know well the other!" Members
the Man of Earth Triad are the gross who must pass through tl
fire of initiation by suitable tests of purification, consecration ar
preparation. Members of the Lovers Triad are the fine who must
tried in matters pertaining to the intellect. Members of the Hern
Triad are the lofty chosen ones in the highest, the elect of tl
A∴A∴, who endure the supreme spiritual tests and ordeals of tl
Illustrious Order of the A∴A∴, that is, the Order of the Silver Sta

Lastly, initiates of the New Order constitute a Religious Body
Free Warriors who, by their might and skill, seek to extend tl
Dominion of the Law of Thelema upon earth. We are dedicated
the magical task of establishing on earth the revolutionary ar
dynamic principles of The Book of the Law. We accept The Boe
of the Law as our Sole Rule of Life, and we are consecrated to t
Spirit of that book and to the Word which it proclaims. The Bo
of the Law is a revelation of paramount importance; it is t

212

preme Link to the Great White Brotherhood by which we may rticipate in the excellent knowledge and lofty administration of e Great Work of the New Aeon of Horus. The Ceremonies of the w Order of the Golden Dawn have been constructed to accord th the revolutionary and dynamic principles of The Book of the w, and they are solely designed to instruct the Candidate in the ysteries of Thelema, for the accomplishment of his True Will, d for the supreme attainment of the Knowledge and Conversion of his Holy Guardian Angel.

The Thelemic Order of the Golden Dawn offers Group and Self-tiation Ceremonies, Classes, Correspondence Lessons, and wsletters to interested aspirants. For further information write:

The Thelemic Temple and Order of the Golden Dawn
1626 No. Wilcox Ave. #418
Los Angeles, CA 90028 USA

Love is the law, love under will.

Sir David Cherubim (Frater Superior Chief)
of the Thelemic Order of the Golden Dawn
Los Angeles, March, 1993 e.v.

Some Reflections From 1985-1987

After the initial hysteria died down for the "control" of the olden Dawn, The Israel Regardie Foundation and the Golden awn Temple have slowly moved forward in fulfilling Regardie's sires.

It seems funny now that some "Adepts" demanded that they ive control of the Golden Dawn as a direct right of succession om Dr. Regardie. The joke is that Regardie never claimed to be charge to begin with.

Francis hoped that after his death the Foundation would assure at his work continued to be made available and that I would sure that his psychological perspective would he maintained. He so hoped that no one would take absolute charge except for rposes of administration. Finally he desired that the Golden iwn Correspondence Course would be completed and distributed d that a practical alchemy course would be started by omeone." I believe that we are accomplishing these tasks.

While I was helping Regardie edit *The Complete Golden Dawn stem of Magic* high in the Colorado mountains, we would spend urs discussing many issues. One that stands out in my memory, vas this wretched desire to have someone in charge. What this iled down to, he thought, was "fear of freedom and just plain iness." After observing the anxiety to take control after his death an attest to the fear of freedom. As to laziness I must say tht the ijority of the students of the Golden Dawn are very dedicated d hard workers.

There has only been one report so far of Regardie reincarnating. number of individuals have claimed to have received instruction messages from him. One case in particular is still being vestigated as it was reported by a reliable source who had ormation which only I could have known.

215

A few disparaging comments hve been made about Regardie
knowledge and magical abilities. From our analysis of the intere
in the Golden Dawn this has not been taken very seriously.

Finally I would like to say that I for one am deeply indebted f
Regardie's influence on my life. As my therapist, teacher ar
friend his mercy and severity have provided me with everlastir
love and guidance.

Christopher S. Hyatt, Ph.
November 17, 198
Santa Monica, C

CHAPTER ELEVEN

SOME INTERESTING DOCUMENTS

This section contains facimiles of some interesting documents from the archives of the Israel Regardie Foundation.

The first three include Regardie's letter of introduction from Crowley, and two documents which show that Dr. Regardie was both a 9th Degree in the O.T.O. and a member of A∴A∴. We include them to dispel, once and for all, the controversy and gossip over these issues.

89 Park Mansions,

Knightsbridge, S. W. 1.

June 12th, 1930.

TO ALL WHOM IT MAY CONCERN:

This will introduce Mr. Israel Regardie, who is my Secretary and my confidential agent.

ALEISTER CROWLEY.

Regardie's Letter Of Introduction From Crowley, June 12, 1930.

A∴ A∴

THE OATH OF A PROBATIONER.

I,........Israel Regardie.........., being of sound
mind and body, on this 28th day of October, An I₄,
the Sun in ° of Scorpio, do hereby resolve in
the Presence of......................., a neophyte of
the A∴ A∴. To prosecute the Great Work: which
is, to obtain a scientific knowledge of the nature
and powers of my own being.

May the A∴ A∴ crown the work, lend me of
Its Wisdom in the work, enable me to understand the
work!

Reverence, duty, sympathy, devotion, assiduity,
trust do I bring to the A∴ A∴. and in one year
from this date may I be admitted to the knowledge
and conversation of the A∴ A∴.!

Witness my hand.....Israel Regardie.....

Motto...אהיה נחש להעה..........

Regardie's Probationer Certificate In The A∴A∴

220

A postcard to Regardie from Crowley
(signing himself in code as 729 which is 3^6 or 666).
The postcard opens "T.I.T.H.T.I.",
("Thrice Illuminated, Thrice Holy, Thrice Illustrious"),
the greeting of a high ranking member of the O.T.O. to a fellow
member who holds the 9th Degree.

Some Useful Tables

This section contains a variety of Tables titled as follows:

• The Twelve Ruling Archangels of the Signs.
• The Twelve Lesser Assistant Angels in the Signs.
• The Twelve Angels Ruling the Twelve Houses of the Heavens and the Signs, co-significations thereof.
• The Hebrew names for the Twelve Signs.
• Lord of the Triplicity by Day.
• Lord of the Triplicity by Night.
• The names of the thirty-six angels ruling the decanates of the signs, to which are added the Egyptian decanates as given by Firmicus and Kircher.

These tables are taken directly from the notebook of a Golden Dawn student from the 1930's. In addition to the utility of the information contained in the tables (e.g., the Hebrew names of the Twelve Signs is rarely seen), the reader may find the notebook entries themselves of historical significance.

The Twelve Ruling Archangels of the Signs

Sign	Name of Angel		
♈	יהוה	מלכידאל	Melchidael
♉	יהוו	אסמודאל	Asmodel
♊	יוהה	אמבריאל	Ambriel
♋	הוהי	מוריאל	Muriel
♌	הויה	ורכיאל	Verchiel
♍	ההוי	המליאל	Hamaliel
♎	והיה	זוריאל	Zuriel
♏	וההי	ברכיאל	Barachiel
♐	ויהה	אדוכיאל	Advachiel
♑	היהו	הנאל	Hanael
♒	היוה	כאמבריאל	Cambriel
♓	ההיו	אמניציאל	Amnitziel

The Twelve Ruling Archangels Of The Signs

223

The Twelve Lesser Assistant Angels in the Signs

Sign	Assistant Angel	
♈	שורהיאל	Sarahiel
♉	ארזיאל	Araziel
♊	סראיתל	Saraiel
♋	פכיאל	Pakiel
♌	שרטיאל	Sartiel
♍	שלתיאל	Schaltiel
♎	חדקיאל	Chadkiel
♏	סאיציאל	Saitziel
♐	סמקיאל	Samkiel
♑	סריטיאל	Saritiel
♒	צכמקיאל	Tsakmakiel
♓	וכביאל	Vacabiel

The Twelve Lesser Assistants Angels In The Signs

224

The Twelve Angels
Ruling the 12 Houses of the Heavens, and the Signs, co-significations thereof.

House	Signs	Name of Ruling Angel	
Asc.	♈	אֲיֶהֵל	Ayel
2d	♉	טוּאֵל	Tual
3d	♊	גִיאֵל	Giel
4d	♋	כַעֲאֵל	Caael
5d	♌	עֲוֹאֵל	Oel
6th	♍	וִיאֵל	Viel
7th	♎	יְהֵאֵל	Yahel
8d	♏	סוּסוֹל	Susol
9th	♐	סוּיֶעֶסאֵל	Suissel
10th	♑	כַשְׁנִיעֲיָרה	Casniyayah
11th	♒	אֲנסוֹאֵל	Ansoel
12th	♓	פַשִּׁיאֵל	Pashiel

The Twelve Angels Ruling The Twelve Houses Of The Heavens
And The Signs, Co-Significations Thereof.

225

The Hebrew Names for
The Twelve Signs.

♈	טלה	Telah
♉	שור	Sör
♊	תאומים	Teohmims
♋	סרטן	Sarton
♌	אריה	Aryeh
♍	בתולה	Betulah
♎	מאזנים	Maynayim
♏	עקרב	Oqeb
♐	קשת	Qeshet
♑	גדי	Gadi
♒	דלי	Dali
♓	דגים	Dogim

The Hebrew Names For The Twelve Signs

ign		
♈	סטרעטין	Saturaator
♉	רהידאל	Raydal
♊	סעדש	Saadesch
♋	רעדר	Raadar
♌	סגהם	Sagham
♍	לסלרא	Laslara
♎	תרגבון	Targaton
♏	ביתחון	Bethehon
♐	אהנז	Alnoy
♑	סנדלעי	Saydoloi
♒	עתור	Oour
♓	רמרא	Ramara

Lord Of The Triplicity By Day

227

♈	ספעטטאוי	Spataoy
♉	טוטת	Totes
♊	עוגרמיען	Ogeromaan
♋	עכאל	Ockal
♌	זלברחית	Zilbrachis
♍	ססיא	Sosia
♎	אחודראון	Achodraon
♏	סהקנב	Sahprov
♐	לברמיים	Labramaim
♑	אלויר	Elvin
♒	פלאון	Pelaon
♓	נתדוריגאל	Nisdorigal

Lord Of The Triplicity By Night

228

[From the original notebook]

Here follow the Names of the 36 Angels ruling the Decanates of the Signs, to which are added the Egyptian decanates in the two lists which contain the names as given by Firmicus & Kircher.

Here follow the names of the 36 Angels ruling the Decanates of the Signs, to which are added the Egyptian decanates in the two lists which contain the names as given by Firmicus & Kircher."

Sign	~~Decanate~~ No. of Degree	Planet	Name of Ruling Angel
♈	1	♂	זר
.	2	☉	בההמי
.	3	♀	טנדר
♉	4	☿	ברדמדי
.	5	☽	מנחראי
.	6	♄	סגנון
♊	7	♃	וגרש
.	8	♂	צהדני
.	9	☉	ביתור
♋	10	♀	מתראוש
.	11	☿	יהדע
.	12	☽	אלינכיר
♌	13	♄	וסנהר
.	14	♃	חעי
.	15	♂	צהיבה
♍	16	☉	אננאורה
.	17	♀	יאיהיה
.	18	☿	מספר

230

Angel	Decanates from Firmicus	from Kircher
Yazar	Asican	Aroueris
Belahmi	Senacher	Anubis
Stender	Asentaus	Horus
Bardensi	Asicath	Serapis
Mincharai	Viroaso	Heliconuros
Yeagenon	Aharp	Apophis
Saqash	Theogar	Ptah
Shaldoni	Nerauna	Cyclops
Bichur	Tepisatrra	Titan
Mithraosh	Sothis	Apollum
Rahdōh	Syth	Hecate
Elincir	Thimuis	Mercophte
Luonalar	Aphruimis	Typhon
Zachoi	Sichacer	Perseus
Sahebah	Phaonisie	Nephthe
Ananaorah	Thumis	Isis
Rayleyoh	Thoffhitas	Bi·Osiris
Mispar.	Aphul	Kronos

♎	ר	19	טרסני
"	לך	20	זהרנץ
♏	ל	21	טהדר
"	♂	22	גמוץ
"	☉	23	ינדוהר
♐	♀	24	תרודיאל
"	☿	25	ישרית
♑	☽	26	הרין
"	לך	27	גבוהא
"	ל	28	יסנין
♒	♂	29	איסיה
"	☉	30	אנדיברודיאל
"	♀	31	ספם
♓	☿	32	בדרון
"	☽	33	רודיאל
"	לך	34	הלמי
"	ל	35	ורון
	♂	36	טריך

232

<table>
<tr><td>...arsani</td><td>Sermeuth</td><td>Neuda</td></tr>
<tr><td>...ahranty</td><td>Aherelinus</td><td>Ouiphtä</td></tr>
<tr><td>...eladar</td><td>Arepieu</td><td>Ophivinorio</td></tr>
<tr><td>...omoty</td><td>Sentaur</td><td>Arimaneio</td></tr>
<tr><td>Nindohar</td><td>Tepieruth</td><td>Merotä</td></tr>
<tr><td>Nierodiel</td><td>Servira</td><td>Panotraguo</td></tr>
<tr><td>Misnio</td><td>Ergbus</td><td>Iolmophtä</td></tr>
<tr><td>Tehario</td><td>Sagen</td><td>Somras</td></tr>
<tr><td>Drohah</td><td>Cheuen</td><td>Teraph</td></tr>
<tr><td>Misnin</td><td>Themis</td><td>Iota</td></tr>
<tr><td>Jesiaral</td><td>Epira</td><td>Rhiaphtä</td></tr>
<tr><td>Jiogeditrodiel</td><td>Hornoth</td><td>Monuphtä</td></tr>
<tr><td>...iopam</td><td>Orooe</td><td>Brondeno</td></tr>
<tr><td>...wodion</td><td>Astio</td><td>?</td></tr>
<tr><td>...nodiel</td><td>Tepioabrao</td><td>Proteno</td></tr>
<tr><td>Ballami</td><td>Archatapeio</td><td>Rephan</td></tr>
<tr><td>roron</td><td>Thorpiteri</td><td>Sourut</td></tr>
<tr><td>Satraph.</td><td>Atunbei</td><td>Phelloplomo</td></tr>
</table>

THE HERMETIC TEMPLE AND ORDER
OF THE GOLDEN DAWN

The reorganization of the **Golden Dawn** was one of **Isra** **Regardie's** dreams: to combine the ancient wisdoms with mode thinking and living. To this end he planted many seeds to assu that the Golden Dawn would survive through the inevitable cris that come with the changing of the guard.

The Hermetic Temple and Order of the Golden Dav provides an environment for both the beginning and advanc Student to make direct contact with other Members, to personally initiated, to take part in Temple functions, and to obta individual instruction.

Among the primary methods of the Order is the elevation of knowledge of the Student through **The Golden Dawn Correspo** **dence Course**, authorized by **Dr. Israel Regardie.**

Membership in the Order entitles you to participate in Temp activities and to enroll in the **Golden Dawn Corresponder Course.** Members also receive a **20% discount** on all **New Fal Publications** books and tapes. Additionally, a **Networki Service** is available in which the names of participating groups a individuals are provided to other participants.

The Hermetic Temple and Order of the Golden Dawn stan ready to bring about the dynamic changes necessary for the N Millennium. A modern Golden Dawn Mystery School, combin the ancient wisdoms and mysteries with modern psycholo philosophy, and high technology will be a leading and lasting fo in the New Aeon.

The Hermetic Temple and Order of the Golden Dawn a the **Israel Regardie Foundation** invite you to partake in the bi of a New Age and a New Planet.

For more information about membership write to:

The Hermetic Temple And Order Of The Golden Dawn
655 East Thunderbird
Phoenix, AZ 85022 U.S.A.